Laughter is the best medicine...

...but can it help cure mid-life crisis?

Tom Mullen thinks so! And so will you when you read *Middle Age and Other Mixed Blessings*. These pages contain such truthful, wise, and witty observations as:

- Growing older: "A sure sign of middle age is a sentence which begins... 'when I was a boy...'"
- Grandparenting: "People over fifty, when they care for an active toddler... are like old movies. They are gray, slow motioned, and often break in the middle."
- Keeping up with technology: "Since Jesus wrote only in the sand, we know that God doesn't demand computer literacy for salvation."

Through Mullen's keen humor you'll discover a lot of heart and a lot of faith behind God's profound and wonderful plan for middle-agers.

MIDDLE AGE

& OTHER MIXED BLESSINGS

TOM MULLEN

Fleming H. Revell Company
Tarrytown, New York

Library of Congress Cataloging-in-Publication Data

Mullen, Thomas James, date.
    Middle age and other mixed blessings / Tom Mullen.
        p.   cm.
    ISBN 0-8007-5399-2
    1. Middle aged persons—Religious life. 2. Mullen, Thomas James, 1934–   . I. Title.
BV4579.5.M85   1991
248.8′4—dc20   91-9653
                                                                         CIP

Copyright © 1991 by Tom Mullen
Published by the Fleming H. Revell Company
Tarrytown, New York 10591
Printed in the United States of America

To Charlie and Hideki,
sons-in-law, sons of God,
and fathers of my grandchildren

CONTENTS

Contents

FOREWORD

> We sometimes feel that only wonderful and un-
> usual experiences can be of interest to others; in
> truth, however, our lives are interesting or hum-
> drum not because of the extraordinary things that
> do or do not happen, but because of the way we
> see and respond to the ordinary things that hap-
> pen all the time.

This comment from a source unknown to me illumi-
nates the rare and charming quality of Tom Mullen as a
person and as a writer. After more than four decades of
hobnobbing and working with writers, I have to say that
I have known few who could equal his creative ability in
catching the extraordinary in the ordinary and making it
come alive. What was once said of writer and journalist
Ring Lardner applies equally to the author of this book:
He "has the habit of catching human beings when they
think no one is looking at them."

Middle Age and Other Mixed Blessings captures the humor and the adventure of our adult years. Underscored,
too, are those Christian values that provide meaning and
give zest to our spiritual pilgrimage as we tussle with the
relationships and events that make up our days. But with
Tom Mullen, there is a winsomeness to the tussle . . . a
sense of reality with which we can all identify.

In an earlier book bearing the delightful title *Parables*

for Parents and Other Original Sinners, Tom Mullen set the stage for our understanding of him and of what life is meant to be in the rough-and-tumble, give-and-take of each twenty-four-hour day. Realistically, he writes, "Life together is a picnic, but picnics include ants, warm lemonade, and the sight of the last available table being claimed by somebody else. The intent of this little book is to reflect on such realities, and it starts from the premise that parents and children are able to enjoy each other more if they expect less perfection and accept the picnic for what it is, ants and all."

Almost two thousand years ago a perceptive Greek philosopher and writer said, "For the wise man, every day is a festival." Indeed, each day is a celebration for the Christian whose life is centered in Jesus Christ. But, unfortunately, we are often guilty of taking ourselves too seriously, thereby allowing our world to shrink into a very small, self-centered ball. I once heard Bishop Fulton Sheen say, "The amount of humor that anyone gets out of the world is the size of the world in which he lives." Tom Mullen's world is a big one, as with rare humor and tender sensitivity he tugs at our hearts with exquisite reminders of God at work in our lives.

For the thoughtful reader of *Middle Age and Other Mixed Blessings*, the landscape and horizons of life will expand. There's something about Tom Mullen's style that encourages us to lift our heads and straighten our shoulders as we anticipate the days ahead in our Father's world.

Floyd W. Thatcher

PREFACE

This is a book about middle age. More specifically, it is a devotional book that reflects upon the years between thirty-five and fifty-five from one Christian's point of view.

There is considerable literature about middle age. From it, certain common observations emerge that are shared by those of us who make it that far.

We begin to worry more about health and physical deterioration because our bodies warn us, sometimes by a kick in the groin. Middle-aged people reflect more on *meaning* in life because they have to deal with transitions, some of them hard to accept. We see our children marry and our parents die. If we have claimed to be Christian, we discover that applying our faith to the circumstances of middle age is still hard, even though we should be more spiritually mature than when we were twenty-five.

This little book, then, is a reflection on middle age based on personal experience. Because most people my age experience ups and downs that are similar, others—I hope—can identify with my stories. Nonetheless, the reader will have to reflect on his or her own journey because mine is peculiar and, at best, can only trigger another person's musings.

It's like the old joke about a husband who comes home from work early and finds a man hiding under his bed. "What are you doing here?" he cries. The reply: "Everybody has to be somewhere." So, my reflections about the experience of middle age are those of a man who is in a specific place. I'm a Quaker, married for thirty-three years to the same woman, father of four grown children, grandparent of one (two, by the time this book is published), seminary teacher at Earlham School of Religion, and part of a larger ecumenical Christian community that has shaped my faith and attitudes toward life.

I conclude that middle age is far better than being dead and, in fact, provides an excellent time frame for serendipities. The blessings are there, and they're undeserved because God is good.

I'm grateful to *Quaker Life*, the denominational publication of Friends United Meeting, for permission to reprint several of my essays that first appeared there. Stan Banker and Jim Newby, editors of the journal in recent years, should not be blamed.

Phyllis Wetherell, Sue Kern, and Merci Townsend

typed early drafts of certain essays. They are three-fifths of the best secretarial staff in the world, and one day I plan to write a book about them, if various legal obstacles can be overcome.

Sarah Northrop, my computer-whiz daughter, typed the entire final draft and offered numerous suggestions to make it better. A woman who can be a church secretary, work for a law firm, give quality care to Chad, encourage her husband, and still find time to bring this book from her father's longhand to clear English on white paper is remarkable. And she works cheap.

If you have read any of my other books, and over eleven Americans have, you've met our family. They continue to provide an excellent laboratory for applying the Christian faith, as well as unending encouragement to me.

The middle-aged years of our family's life together have seen our tribe increase. Charles and Hideki married Sarah and Martha, respectively, and they have enriched our lives and provided Nancy and me with grandchildren. To be able to love the people your children marry as much as you love your children is an undeserved blessing. So this book is dedicated to Charlie and Hideki. May their tribe increase because it's my tribe, too.

PART I
REMINDERS

Middle age reminds us that if we're technically not yet old, we're absolutely no longer young.

Bodies forty-five or older send messages. Until about age thirty, we experience anabolism—the process of getting bigger, stronger, and healthier. By about age thirty-five, the process has reversed and catabolism takes over. Large words, such as *catabolism*, need no definition other than a mirror or the annual physical exam.

After age forty-five, the physical signs of catabolism appear regularly. For example, during a routine physical exam I complained to the doctor about recurring gastritis and the need for frequent nocturnal visits to the bathroom. He asked how old I was. I told him. He said, "You're right on schedule. You're on the down side of middle age." Thanks, doc, you unmade my day.

Worrying over your health can dominate your

thoughts, until you realize the house is empty because the kids have grown up and moved away. True, much of their stuff is still stored in seldom-used bedrooms, and they call on the phone—often collect—a lot.

But it's quiet, and out of the silence come memories. We recall our oldest daughter's comment when she was twelve and she and her younger sister were away from the other two children with us. Sarah remarked, "It's nice having just the *original* family together."

She was premature. When the nest empties, only then is the *original* family present. A husband and wife have each other, easy access to the bathroom, and high phone bills. It's a new day!

The emptying process takes place over years, but it is focused when the family dog dies. Young married people with small children acquire dogs, cats, gerbils, guinea pigs, goldfish, and occasionally a leopard. The pets come and go along the way.

One day, however, the nest is empty and only the family dog remains. Given the ability of canine creatures to win the affection of otherwise rational adults, the dog becomes the center rather than the periphery of attention. When it dies after eighteen years of being in the way, one more reminder has been issued that life is in a new phase.

The temptation to do things the way you've always done them is deep and wide. Younger colleagues and your own grown-up children, for example, are evangelists for computers, word processors, and software. Until they confront you, the only disc you've noticed is the one in your back that slipped. To become computer literate after age fifty is more than twice as hard as when you're twenty-five. How does one adjust without sacrificing a lifelong commitment to the instrument God intended humans to use—the ballpoint pen?

In other words, the pace of life is discovered to have changed. Middle age provides intimations of mortality. We think more often about retirement. We reflect about the meaning of what we do rather than how successful we are. We conclude that status is far less important than relationships. Enjoying the company of those sharing the journey is as important as the destination.

Here's the good news! The reminders are not necessarily warnings. From a Christian perspective, in fact, they are opportunities. And the only problem with middle age is that, when opportunity knocks, it takes longer to answer the door.

1

SHAPING UP

Middle age is when we're too young to go on Social Security and too old to get a better job. We can still do everything we used to do, but not until tomorrow. It takes longer to rest than it does to get tired. Those of us wearing bifocals step off every curb as if we're testing water in a pool. Middle age is when you don't have to own antiques to sit on something that's fifty years old.

Even so, unless we have a debilitating health problem, we keep thinking that in a week or two we'll feel as energetic as ever. We still may be go-getters but now it takes two trips. Aging is like a neighborhood gossip. It tells on us. The temptation is to throw up our hands and let our bodies decay.

Two factors prevent most middle-agers from giving in to the inevitable. One, it hurts to raise our arms that high, and, two, most of us over fifty are married. A spouse dedicated to getting her husband in shape will accept no excuses and applies pressure that makes the Spanish Inquisition seem wimpish by comparison.

"Now, Tom," says Nancy when we have a discussion about my need for more exercise, "I read an article that says certain types of workouts will measurably help your heart."

Before I can roll over on the couch, she quotes from the article:

> The best kinds of activities are those exercises that use major muscles repeatedly, but at a steady level below maximum capacity. These include jogging, running, swimming, and bicycling. Brisk walking, rowing, rope-skipping, and running in place also produce specific physiological changes. Such exercises should be performed at least four times a week, preferably more.

The determination in her voice is genuine, so I resort to one of my best strategies—avoidance. "Honey, you're right," I say. "I do need more exercise. But I hate jogging, running, and rope-skipping. And you know that when I swim, I tend to sink. And my bicycle tires are flat. How about if I play racquetball with Dick Davis a couple of times a week? Playing games is fun, and—"

"The fact is," responds the woman who thirty-three years ago promised to love me and rub my back after exercise, "you and Dick are seldom in town at the same time and when you do play, it takes a week for you to recuperate. The article says *regular* exercise at a *steady* level below *maximum* capacity. Let's go for a brisk two-mile walk before breakfast and in a little while your cardiovascular system will be humming like a new car."

Since our new car at that moment was in the garage for a tune-up, her metaphor was strained. However, because I had promised in 1957 to love her and dry the dishes, I agreed. Besides, we'd tried early-morning exercise before, and it had never lasted longer than three weeks.

Brisk walking at 6:15 A.M. has its merits. One feels self-disciplined and self-righteous as he strides along, swinging his arms as if cutting holes in the air. Nancy is happy, convinced she is saving my life. And the neighbors, who are just getting up as we return from our walk, are impressed, possibly jealous.

Had we settled for brisk walking, all would have been well, particularly after the second week, when the pain in my legs no longer seemed greater than my desire to live. We were walking farther and feeling better. It was then that the Science of Nutrition entered our lives.

Once again, it was a magazine article that invaded my tranquility. I should have promised to start exercising if Nancy would agree to stop reading. It was, however, too late.

Since we are both diabetics and can't eat much of anything that tastes good, nutrition for the sake of muscle tone was as welcome as water to a drowning man. Most diets, after all, are constructed around food you detest. We can be sure that our "nutritional plan" will center around cottage cheese and celery. And it will never—repeat, never—include french fries.

So, whether it is the Rockefeller diet—a misnomer since it contains nothing rich—or the Weight Watchers diet, which is a form of starving to death in order to live longer, a "nutritional plan" will accompany an exercise program as surely as gas pains follow baked beans. Each diet is endorsed by either celebrities or athletes who finished no lower than third in the Olympic tryouts.

They lied. They made it sound easy, and it wasn't. They promised I could eat food I liked in small portions. Small, however, is larger than tiny, and dinner music has more calories than our "nutritional plan."

Eventually we compromised. We settled on a diet, without desserts, good for diabetics that did not require the discipline of Gandhi to follow. It took a pound of willpower to starve off a few ounces of calories, but we devoured enough food to complete our early-morning walks.

Getting in shape when married is easier because helping each other is an act of love. Nancy, a diabetic since age ten, has had to eat healthfully all her life. She views good health as a form of stewardship, and she is right. Being overweight shortens life. It is as if God summons us after we've eaten our share in less time than we should.

Just as we are tempted to deny the signs of aging, so do we resist paying the price of good health such as exercise and nutrition. We buy a bathroom scale that lies, or we deliberately hang out with people in worse shape than we are. Somewhere in the middle of middle age, we decide to take care of our bodies or we don't.

That moment of truth, like so many others, has a biblical base. In John 5:6–8, Jesus confronted a man who had been lying by the pool of Bethesda for a long time. He had been ill for thirty-eight years, so it was clear he was in mid-life. Jesus asked him, "Do you want to be healed?" The man offered his excuses, not unlike the ones I've used to avoid exercise and diets. In reply, Jesus essentially told him to get off his duff (a loose translation) and walk.

Jesus didn't insist that he walk briskly, swinging his arms, nor that it be done early in the morning. And nowhere does He demand that we follow a diet so rigid we're forced to survive on cottage cheese and celery. But we know that the temptation in middle age to choose death (bodily decline) rather than face life with self-discipline is real. So His question for those of us over fifty is direct. Do we want to be whole? Middle age is not the beginning of the end. It is the end of the beginning.

We still have miles to go before we sleep. And an unending supply of celery.

2
HARDENED ARTERIES

Playing intramural basketball at age fifty-four has prompted a variety of reactions. Some of my opponents of ESR's team, Yahweh's Warriors, show respect, nay, awe when they realize they are one-third my age. Others demonstrate overt fear, and one undergraduate admitted it! "Tom, I'm really afraid you're going to be hurt!"

Twenty years ago such a challenge would have caused my adrenaline to flow and inspire fresh, vigorous effort on my part. Now my adrenaline just lies there, and I am reduced to snorting incoherent mumbles having to do with "young whippersnappers" and "no respect for age." My teammates encourage me, however, remarking that they have never before seen jump shots taken with both feet on the floor.

My presence on the floor influences the strategy of

the game. Our opponents fast-break, casually dribble around my slow-motion efforts to guard them, and try to keep the ball away from our players. Our team, except for me, hustles back on defense—and tries to keep the ball away from me.

It is a painful experience for an aging Hoosier to realize the end of his playing days is near. (Objective observers have noted that the end came some years ago. Only the realization has been recent.) But let's face it, the time had come to hang up the sneakers.

When your wife checks your insurance coverage before every game and the school nurse shows up only on the nights you play, the handwriting is on the gymnasium wall. When fifteen-foot shots travel thirteen feet on the average, it matters not whether you win or lose, but only if you survive the game. The time to retire had come.

The decision came gradually. Growing older, after all, takes time. Nonetheless, the awareness builds that a once young, vibrant mare or stallion, as the case may be, is not what she or he used to be. What was once (at least in one's mind) a sleek, smooth-running machine now shows signs of used-car-ness.

I noticed that my skin is drier and a little thinner, and tiny blood vessels show through. The days of a pink, ruddy complexion are past, and in fact I sometimes look purple.

The pigment in my hair continues to disintegrate and is replaced by air, which causes it to turn gray. Nature provides an inherent contradiction: I am older and the-oretically wiser but more an airhead than ever!

Occasionally my prostate glands swell and block off the end of the bladder. Thus, nocturnal habits include frequent visits to the bathroom. Should I forget my an-tiquity and eat pizza after eleven o'clock at night, the visits increase and remind me that the old cast-iron stomach has rusted.

I have what is called "frozen shoulders," too, causing me to whimper slightly each time I tuck my shirt into the back of my pants. Every morning of my life I eat oat bran to reduce my cholesterol and lengthen my life. Whether eating oat bran every day actually lengthens life, I do not know, but it seems longer.

People older than I provide helpful advice that just over the horizon (or should we say "over the hill") await gallstones, arthritis, and sagging jowls. Fortunately, they say, we won't think about them much since our memory is fading because of the wearing out of brain cells!

Nature provides many clues that everything has its season and all life moves toward death. Giving up bas-ketball or changing an eating habit goes with the terri-tory. Growing older is an inconvenience, but it surely beats the alternative.

Living temperately is one lesson we learn, but there is another, less obvious one as well. Chronological age may bring us problems with our liver, pancreas, and knee joints, but it ought also to bring us spiritual maturity. The qualities of compassion, forgiveness, and awareness of God's grace should improve, not diminish, with age.

It doesn't always happen. Age may bring spiritual hardening of the arteries. Age may increase self-centeredness, and we sometimes discover we have a heart problem a doctor can't fix. If we don't grow in wisdom and stature, and particularly in favor with God, then our souls can become as decrepit as our bodies.

So when our outside shots fall short and gastritis follows pizza as surely as autumn follows summer, there is a double message: May we live temperately for the sake of our bodies and compassionately for the sake of our souls.

Lower back pain may be an inevitable consequence of aging, but heartfelt concern for God and neighbor is not. And that contemporary philosopher Yogi Berra could have been referring to spiritual growth when he said, "It's never over till it's over." That's the main difference between basketball and life.

3

JUST AS I AM, WITHOUT ONE FLEA

Terry, the dog, followed our daughter home from school one day and was allowed to stay "until we could find out who owned her." In short order we discovered who owned *us*, as she delivered puppies in our basement one week after arriving and not even Jack the Ripper would turn a new mother out into the cold.

I tried to address rationally and logically the problems of owning a dog. Rationality and logic, however, have nothing to do with animals, particularly when your wife sides with the children. Nor do commands or ultimatums make any difference. "Either the dog goes or I go!" I proclaimed. As the family weighed their choices, I withdrew the offer.

Terry stayed for eighteen years. When finally she died, the whole family wept. The first Christmas without her was strangely deficient. The children had insisted that gifts (dog biscuits and rubber bones) be included each Christmas for Terry, and we faithfully hung a stocking for her over the fireplace. After her death she was conspicuous by her absence. The old joke, "Freedom comes when the children leave home and the dog dies," didn't fit. Thus, this essay explores the important theological question, "Why do dogs become so important to people?" Why do we regard them as nearly human, converse with them as if they can understand, and mourn their passing when they die?

Probably not on their merits. There may be high-class dogs who are consistently obedient and win prizes for "best of breed." Family dogs, however, become the center of attention for a different reason—they are invariably in the way! They are outside when they should be in, and inside when they belong out. Neighbors call when your dog chases their cat or upsets their garbage can. When inside, the typical family dog is either asleep in a doorway or on the new sofa, rubbing the vestiges of decayed fish into the fabric.

Nor are most family dogs loved for their beauty. Terry was part spitz, part terrier, mostly mutt. She was short and round with a broad, flat back. She looked like a tan coffee table. Her legs were slightly bowed because she was overweight. He face had a perpetual look of melancholy which inspired pity which led to continual gifts which led to her being overweight with bowed legs. Terry's tail wagged constantly, so much so that one of the children declared that she was a story with a happy ending! Beautiful, however, she was not.

Dogs, furthermore, complicate family life because of human affection for them. Terry was once missing for twelve hours. Our entire family, several neighbors, and teams of Earlham students searched the campus and eight city blocks. She was finally found in a neighbor's garage, the door of which had blown shut after Terry had entered to forage among their trash. Once discovered—nay rescued—she was indignant, as if we should have found her sooner.

Happy, tail-wagging dogs knock over the good crystal on the coffee table. Should they stay in their own yards, as they're supposed to, they dig holes in the flower beds. Adults lecture them as if they were people: "Terry, do not leap on Ruth when she's wearing her good dress." "Terry, you are not to lap water out of the toilet." When we arrived home after a trip, Nancy would tell me to go into the house, find Terry, and give her a lecture about being good.

So why do we put up with dogs who cost money, complicate life, disobey, and make us feel guilty if we fail to cater to their whims? Terry was an unnecessary expense, a nuisance, and frequently acted unseemly by either human or canine standards. Why do we mourn a nuisance?

Perhaps it's because dogs provide humans with adoring esteem. We know we do not possess those qualities that set us apart from others, that command respect and allegiance. To regard ourselves as worthy of praise and deserving of adoration is both immodest and unQuakerly.

Family dogs don't care about our status. However hopeless, however incompetent we are, whether we're children or adults, dogs still admire us, love us, and forgive us. As the world buffets us, as we face defeat and discouragement, the family dog cares for us just the same.

Therefore, as much as we'd like to be free of their tyranny, as much as we'd prefer they be better looking and better behaved, dogs like Terry accept us as we are—faults included—and we welcome them in our lives. They love unconditionally, like God. Maybe that's why the poet, Francis Thompson, referred to God as "The Hound of Heaven." Or, to paraphrase a hymn, to be loved unconditionally is to be loved "just as I am, without one flea." In the eyes of a dog, there is no higher status.

4

JESUS WROTE IN THE SAND

Parents introduce their children to technology. They teach them to ride a bicycle, use a sewing machine, and—under duress—drive a car.

However, certain uses of technology are not a natural extension of lessons parents have taught. They are peculiar to generations younger than middle age because the technology did not exist thirty-five years ago.

Computer technology is a case in point. While many middle-aged folks use computers and word processors, they were not brought up with them as their children have been. A whole generation of young adults are as comfortable using computers as they were sleeping with stuffed animals when they were children. Students arrive at college with hardware, printers, and software they have been using since the sixth grade.

At Christmas, advertisers send subtle messages to

parents that they are unfit if they don't provide their kindergarteners with computer programs that will teach them the history of civilization by age seven. An Apple IIe is plugged into a third grader's room next to the night-light.

When we were children, we went to summer camp. We memorized the books of the Bible and played softball and daydreamed about the opposite sex. Now children go to computer camp and hug, not snuggy bear, but software to their bosoms during horizontal time.

Thus it is a shock to the nervous system of a father, once regarded as a veritable font of knowledge by his children, to realize they know all about computers while he knows nothing. He doesn't even understand their conversations.

To illustrate, consider the following exchange between two of my daughters. Sarah designed a billing program for the law office where she works, and her sister Ruth would no more compose an article with pen and paper than a non-Amish farmer would plow with a horse.

Sarah: To make your text look just the way you want, put your cursor on it and click your mouse in the style you want.

Ruth: Notice that another toggle switches between the layout mode, which is faster than the straight text entry but doesn't show the formatting.

They were discussing the merits of a word processor that will do everything but pop corn. However, to their father, who is convinced that if God had wanted us to use word processors, God would not have invented ballpoint pens, their dialogue was incomprehensible. I was brought up to believe it was wrong to be a curser, and I have never desired to click a mouse. And toggle switches between layout modes sound vaguely obscene.

Even so, the gap between generations could possibly be bridged were it not for the evangelical zeal of the daughters to convert their father.

"Dad, my computer [editorial note: paid for by the father] provides excellent control over typeface, size, leading, and indentation."

"And my word processor," her sister proclaims, "contains a powerful spell checker and a thesaurus that provides both synonyms and definitions."

Then, in unison, like witnesses for the prosecution, they plead, "Dad, I can't believe you won't learn how to use a computer!"

Ruth adds, "I was embarrassed when you couldn't use the electronic reference file at Lilly Library yesterday. What if one of my friends had been there?"

As I sputter my disclaimers about being too busy and how the old card file system worked fine, a look of dismay—nay, pity—clouds their eyes. "Dad," intones Sarah, "I know lots of people even older than you who use computers."

She's right, of course. Many men and women my age

have betrayed our generation and in pathetic attempts to recapture lost youth also evangelize for computer usage. One of my colleagues argues more passionately for investing in Macintosh computers than he does for converting pagans to Christianity. And he is a theologian who knows better than most the connection between the apple and the fall!

To be treated as a technological leper by one's children and an academic Neanderthal by colleagues is a heavy burden. Its humiliation is surpassed only when your wife of thirty-three years agrees with THEM.

"Now, Tom," she says, in the voice last used when teaching first graders to tie their shoes, "you must keep an open mind. You obviously have computer anxiety, so I want you to enroll in this workshop."

The woman I married for better or worse then thrusts a brochure into my sweaty palms. My vision, blurred by tears of rejection, reveals that the workshop is titled "Computer Learning for Cowards" and hints that resistance is subliminal castration fear.

It is in that moment that I realize my resistance is theological, not technological. True, it is heightened by lifelong incompetence around anything mechanical, including can openers. But I know I can learn to use a computer, and certainly I covet the respect of my children and the love of my wife even though she left out "obey" in our wedding vows.

Theologically, however, we must retain the essence of our being. A middle-aged dog *can* learn new tricks, but once in a while he must draw a line to preserve his freedom. We have to say, "Here I sit, pen in hand. I can do no other."

It is not necessarily a noble stand nor a rational one. But it is a stand I can take which by its very stubbornness identifies me as unwilling to be tossed to and fro by every wind of doctrine.

A case, albeit a weak one, can be made against computers, and I will win an occasional rhetorical victory. THEY will push the wrong button every so often and lose six months of material. I can carry my pad and pen in a briefcase while THEY will have to rent a U-Haul to transport their equipment.

But, as I said, my case is theological. Middle age allows us an occasional idiosyncrasy. Those of us who have been through three revivals of the wide necktie are entitled to be stubborn about some things. I've chosen computers.

Since Jesus wrote only in the sand, we know that God doesn't demand computer literacy for salvation. Descartes said, "I think. Therefore I am." This middle-aged man says, "I write—longhand on lined sheets of paper—therefore I am—stubborn!"

Amen. (Translation: "So may it be.")

5

THE EMPTY NEST

About the time we get the hang of being parents, our children grow up and leave home. For years their needs dominate our lives, and one day we discover they've finished college, taken jobs, and stopped bringing home their laundry.

It's an important moment. It defines a new set of circumstances for parents who—let's be honest—have longed for this day to arrive. *At last,* we think, *we will be free from their intrusions into our peace, tranquility, and bank accounts.*

When children are small, they demand attention. Every child's first tooth, first day of school, or first romance is an EVENT. Rookie parents commemorate each EVENT with appropriate pomp and circumstance. Pictures are taken of baby on bear rugs and on rugs bare. The refrigerator may be empty, but its door is the official display case for report cards and memorabilia honoring everything from a red ribbon for cookie baking at the county fair to best breed in the dog show.

When our children were tiny, the most-used piece of baby furniture we had was the playpen—Nancy would often sit in it so the children couldn't reach her. During the 4-H years, their leader-mother was continually going to or coming from meetings, while the eldest daughter tried out her food preparation experiments on her father. Such activities taught independence, as many mothers learned to change tires and many fathers learned how to cook.

Little League and girl's softball ran our lives for several years. Those Americans who worry about Communists or other sinister forces taking away their freedom are well-advised to investigate, instead, all organized sports for children. Two children in two leagues can totally control evenings, mealtimes, and family vacations. Parents learn too late that it was in The Big Inning that God's plan for creation was laid out.

Teenage years produce their own peculiar threats to an orderly, civilized life-style. Teenagers dominate space, ignore time, and march to the tune of a different drummer—usually by way of headphones surgically attached to the ears. They are often found sprawling on, sitting cross-legged in the way, stretched out beside, or late getting to. Parents of teenagers fluctuate between high hopes for the future of the world and total despair for civilization as we've known it.

Then, one day, the nest is empty. Of course, children-become-adults do not suddenly disappear. They never slice the umbilical cord neatly and cleanly but stretch it until, frayed and worn, it breaks. And a broken umbilical cord means two sets of people are in a different place in life.

Much of the difference is pleasurable. When the children are gone, a father can walk right into the bathroom like a real person. No longer will he have to knock and plead for a chance to take a shower sometime in the same century. The telephone will ring and the call will be for him. Parents can drive their own car without checking first to see which daughter's life will be permanently damaged if transportation to a Meaningful Place to meet a Significant Other is not available.

When the nest is empty, a husband can kiss his wife squarely on the lips without having one of his progeny turn eyes heavenward and moan, "Daaaad. . . !" Parents can go away for a weekend without leaving notes all over the house with instructions that are either unnecessary ("The ice cream is in the freezer") or futile ("Please clean up the kitchen").

Most of all, the empty nest is quiet. When children are there, quiet is a sure sign of trouble. When our son was small, Nancy would listen carefully and then say, "Tom, go find Brett and tell him to stop!" Post-children quiet is warm and comfortable, safe and peaceful.

Sociologists warn that when children leave home, the relationship between husband and wife is tested.

Maybe, but raising them to adulthood strengthens a relationship in the process, not unlike the way a common enemy unites a nation during wartime.

More often, an empty nest enables parents to reflect upon the child-raising experience. Few families grow up together without both pain and joy, both satisfaction and wondering how things could have been better. After twenty or thirty years of parenting, survivors recognize an important truth: Family life is a picnic and picnics include ants, warm lemonade, and unscheduled cloudbursts.

From the quietness of the empty nest, parents can realize the adventure was worth it. They can accept the picnic for what it is, ants and all. In fact, they do well to savor the moments they have, for some children-become-adults return home again, certainly to visit, possibly to live. And I'm told, they often bring children of their own.

Hallelujah! The place was too quiet, and whenever your children produce children of their own, Scripture is fulfilled. We refer to that passage which says, " 'Vengeance is mine,' says the Lord!" Amen.

6
DISAPPOINTING THE FUNERAL DIRECTOR

A tombstone inscription reads: "I expected this but not just yet." In mid-life most of us think about retirement a lot and death a little. It goes with the territory.

Younger adults seldom ponder the distant future, and most of us are past middle age before we admit we're in it. One of my relatives refuses to tell people she's fifty-two, even though it makes her children illegitimate. At some point, however, we face reality and think about the future. We conclude not that our time is up, but that our time is short.

Sociologists argue that ten years before retirement is when we begin to anticipate it. Our contributions to a pension or retirement plan have been disappearing from our paychecks for years, but at about age fifty-five we pay attention to the mathematics of our future.

Pastors who live in church-owned houses have to

think about a place of their own. Women who never worked outside the home investigate their spouse's pension plan and wonder, *Will it be enough?* All those good folks who have looked forward to retirement trips to Paris or shuffleboard matches in a Florida trailer park begin to ask hard financial questions.

Those of us fortunate enough to work for employers who provide pensions and investment plans for rainy days may find it's wetter than we thought. Our planning for rainy days was foresighted, we thought, but we didn't know the supermarket and the gas station would keep seeding the clouds.

Retirement is when our take-home pay makes the trip on its own. Social Security taxes, which are exorbitant when we pay them, seem meager when we draw upon them. Social Security benefits are to retirement what prunes are to old age. They barely keep us going. And the cost of health care is like blood pressure. Just thinking about it causes it to rise.

This essay, however, is not about good, better, and best financial planning for retirement. Wise middle-aged people will do it, but insurance companies, labor unions, and government agencies can complicate that issue for us without any help.

Nor is this essay about writing a will, even though failure to have a will is a popular form of denying our mortality. In fact, we can sympathize with the person whose last will and testament simply read, "Being of sound mind, I spent it all while I was alive." At least he accepted the fact that he couldn't take it with him to the grave.

Instead, this essay is about encountering our finitude. Retirement and death are simply occasions for doing so. Dr. Elisabeth Kübler-Ross argues that we are well-advised if we're able to discuss death and dying as an intrinsic part of life, just as pregnant women and their husbands freely discuss birth. She says that we can deal with death better when it is still "miles away" than when it is "right in front of the door."

By middle age our bodies provide plenty of reminders of life's finitude so that it is in the back of our minds whether or not we speak about it aloud. Since Nancy has been a diabetic since age ten, she has had to face its implications all her life. Therefore, she has deeply held feelings about one of the possibilities that go with diabetes, namely, spending her final weeks or months on artificial life supports. She wants no part of such efforts. Thus, a television show, a movie like *Steel Magnolias*, or a Sunday school discussion will trigger her opinions. I've heard them so often, in fact, that I refer to her speech as "Pulling the Plug 101." "Promise me, Tom," she'll say as we're having dinner, "that you'll just let me die. Give me painkillers, but please don't hook me up to a machine that drips fluid into my comatose body and makes 'beep beep' noises I can't even hear. . . . Would you please pass the potatoes."

I am able to agree with her intellectually. Yet, I find it easier to choose that course of action for myself than for her. After all, I've grown quite fond of her over the years and spent a lot of money getting her teeth fixed. But it's clear she is serious, and no one can accuse her of denying her mortality.

Since I expect to live to age ninety and die at the hand of a jealous husband, artificial life supports do not generate my passions. My concern is the way we deny death by our funeral ceremonies. Having attended many funeral services, I am troubled by words and practices that reject the reality of grief and death. "He's not dead. He's just sleeping in the arms of God," intoned one pastor at the funeral of a friend. "She's gone to a far better place," said another, leaving the impression we should be tickled pink by the prospect.

Therefore, Nancy has to listen to my speech about the kind of memorial service I want. Wearing my best suit, stretched out in a box as if sleeping with my glasses on, while spectators walk by with sad faces is a scene I'd prefer to avoid. Thus a medical school will get our bodies, and the plan is to have a memorial service followed by an open house with refreshments. I hope a good crowd will attend (that's why there will be refreshments). I'd like my loved ones and friends to say a few words, possibly exaggerate my virtues, sing a couple of hymns, and laugh and cry together.

Our children hate to hear either of us discuss such matters, as it upsets them. When they reach middle age, however, it will be a more comfortable topic. I'm convinced that our ability to contemplate our finitude is directly connected to the quality of our Christian faith. A shallow or nominal faith is often useless when we contemplate death. Deeply religious people accept death as the natural end of life. Christians grieve, of course, but not as those without hope.

The irony is that death is easier to plan for than retirement. Both are preoccupations of middle age, but neither has to be morbid. The gift that comes when we are able to anticipate the end things of our lives is that we are free to get on with the business of joyful living. Once we've made our plans, we can live in such a way that, when we die, even the funeral director will be disappointed.

Part II
Celebrations

Certain events can be celebrated only after you've reached middle age.

Being present for your oldest daughter's wedding is a unique blessing. We see one of God's intentions fulfilled.

The father of the bride may try to remember his own wedding day, but one lesson middle age teaches is that nostalgia isn't what it used to be. Parents hear their children saying their vows and realize they were never that young, that naïve, that fresh. Given the exposure to knowledge, both carnal and spiritual, that young adults acquire growing up in America, they *aren't* that innocent or naïve.

Nevertheless, witnessing God's creation of a new family is an undeserved blessing available to fathers and mothers of the bride and groom. As your child unites with another "for better or worse," until death separates them, you experience Grace.

In fact, middle age provides an understanding of how to celebrate life with special meaning. Some weddings are not spiritual experiences; they are commercial extravaganzas. Parents succumb to the temptation to do the wedding right (translation: expensively), much to the delight of photographers, clothing manufacturers, caterers, and limousine rentals all over America.

Middle-aged Christians have a chance to celebrate holidays without having to impress others or go bankrupt. They have learned that it really is the thought, not the gift, that counts at Christmas. And, thank you very much, frenetic partying on New Year's Eve is as welcome as popcorn to a thirsty man. A kinder, gentler celebration will do just fine.

Another unexpected blessing that occasionally comes to Christians forty-five or older is seeing the fruits of preaching, teaching, and nurturing that parents have offered their children over the years. If, as it seems, fathers and mothers carry responsibility for the sins they have visited upon their progeny, it's only fair they celebrate the virtues of their sons and daughters as well.

Thus, when our second daughter chose to marry a wonderful man with many virtues, who happened to be Japanese, it was a special joy to see that Martha had transcended the cultural and racial biases that limit most Americans. In Christ there really is no East or West.

When a child practices purity of heart, she helps her father see God.

Another event available only to those who have lived long enough to celebrate it is the birth of a grandchild. Had we known how grand grandparenting would be, we'd have grown older faster! Having a child makes a man out of the father and a boy out of the grandfather.

Our grandchild has only one fault. He needs brothers, sisters, or cousins. We take pictures, bore the neighbors, delight even in his burps, and thank God daily for a small creature no grown-up, middle-aged, otherwise mature person could ever be good enough to deserve.

For middle-class parents, putting children through college is the American dream. When your youngest child graduates, however, emotions are mixed. There is anxiety as the father wonders how to invest the thousands no longer committed to tuition. And there is wonder, too, as the parent tries to figure out why his children continue to ask for advice when each one did better in college than he did.

Mostly, however, there is satisfaction. The Bible says we are to love God with our minds—as well as hearts and souls—so education is a form of stewardship. And as your youngest daughter stands in her cap and gown, clutching her diploma, and hugging strangers, your cup runneth over as you say, sweetly, "Don't just stand there. Start supporting yourself."

When your own brother turns sixty, and he's less than four years your senior, a psychological clock begins to tick. We know that one's place in the family affects one's role in the family as well. The oldest is usually the yardstick by which siblings measure their progress. That's why the prodigal's behavior so upset his father and older brother. He broke the pattern.

However determinedly I cling to the belief that fifty-six is part of middle age, when my brother thoughtlessly turns sixty, it's time for a reality check. The clear message is that brothers—and sisters, parents, and colleagues—cannot delay telling their families they're loved.

So, Frank's now old and I'm close, but a sixtieth birthday is a time to celebrate. Call it sibling revelry.

7
FATHER OF THE BRIDE

On June 27, 1982, our daughter Sarah was married in a Quaker wedding. Weddings after the manner of Friends are different from most other Protestant services. After some introductory words by a pastor or clerk, the entire gathering sits in silence. Eventually the bride and groom stand and repeat their vows to each other. They then seat themselves and sign their wedding certificate.

A period of open worship follows, out of which individuals may say a prayer, offer words of counsel, or even sing a song. A member of the wedding party then reads the wedding certificate aloud, and after the service is completed all are invited to sign the certificate as evidence of their support and presence. A committee of elders, which may or may not include clergy, has oversight of the Meeting for Worship.

This essay recalls the internal reflections of the father of the bride—his oldest daughter and the first of his four children to marry.

"Friends, this is indeed a happy and joyous occasion. We have all come here today to share our blessing with Sarah and Charles as they exchange their wedding vows. No other human covenant is more sacred, no other vows more important . . ."

Max makes a great clerk of their marriage committee. He's good with words and, let's face it, he looks like a Quaker should look, with the beard and plain dress. The beard conceals the fact he isn't wearing a necktie, but Nancy's Presbyterian relatives will surely notice. Just wait until everybody settles into silence. Her Uncle Paul will think somebody forgot his lines.

"In the presence of God, and these our Friends, I take thee, Sarah, to be my wife, promising with Divine assistance to be unto thee a loving and faithful husband . . ."

That did it. Nancy has become Niagara Falls. No need to go there for a honeymoon. Sarah and Charlie can stay at home and watch the mother of the bride cry. She didn't cry twenty-five years ago when she married me. She smiled and laughed a lot. She even blew in my ear when we kissed. How much Sarah looks like her mother. No wonder Charlie loves her. He really does love her. They're going to make it.

"In the presence of God, and these our Friends, I take thee, Charles, to be my husband, promising . . ."

Women are lucky. Everybody expects them to cry at weddings, but fathers are supposed to sit like stones and smile heroically. Hey, I helped that young woman grow up. When she had eye surgery, I sat in her hospital room all night. I used to rock her to sleep. And now she's going to get married. I feel like going over to her, grabbing her around the knees, and yelling, "He's taking away my baby!" I guess I won't do that, though. I guess I'll cry—in a manly way, of course.

"Marriage is a sharing of lives and values. It is looking outwardly in the same direction. It is embracing the world while embracing each other. Those of us who know Sarah and Charles are confident . . ."

This is one time I'm glad we're Quakers. Every person who has spoken out of the silence has said words that are just right. Arthur's comments were perfect. He and Hugh were Sarah's favorite teachers at Earlham. Nancy used three Kleenex on Arthur's words alone. Bill's song was original. It would have touched Attila the Hun. I'd like to stand and say something, too. I'm her father after all, and I get leadings, too. . . . What's that, Lord? Sit still and be quiet? This wedding does not need a grown man who blubbers incoherently? Yes, Lord.

"And in further confirmation thereof, they, the said Charles Northrop and Sarah Mullen (she according to the custom of marriage, adopting the surname of her husband) did then and there to these present set their hands . . ."

Signing the certificate always seems awkward to me. Two people, half bent over, carrying a table over to the bride and groom—well, it lacks dignity, particularly when the fountain pen falls to the floor. But it does take courage and nerves of steel. Charlie's hand is shaking so hard we won't be able to read his signature. He might as well be named Rumpelstiltskin! I wonder what it would be like to have a son-in-law named Rumpelstiltskin. "Say, Rump, can you and Sarah come over for dinner next Thursday?"

"Lovely wedding . . . Congratulations! . . . Many years of happiness!"

I understand now why we need both God and friends present for weddings. This whole room is full of love for these two. Look at them. Charlie has just kissed three women in a row. Twenty minutes ago he declared his undying love for my daughter. Sarah's matched him, kiss for kiss. Does she have one left for me? Why would she? I'm only her father. I only brought her up and changed her diapers and paid for the wedding and . . ."

"Thank you, Daddy. It was perfect."

Well, maybe not perfect, but clearly it was blessed by God. And that makes all the difference.

8
INNOCENTS ABROAD

We finally were forced to visit Japan. Our daughter Martha lives there, and besides, Richmond, Indiana, is a community where about half the population has been to Japan nine times.

At least it seems that way, and we suffered from a bad case of travel inferiority, a psychological condition that cosmopolitan neighbors nurture the way a drafty room causes colds.

Well-traveled folk know that the last thing anybody wants to hear is a detailed account of somebody else's safari. Nonetheless, subtle messages get delivered that expose your stick-in-the-mud existence for what it is.

They speak of exotic restaurants in Tokyo; you talk of making your own Mexican tortilla at Rax's. They accidentally flash a 1,000-yen bill while paying the tab; you think it's their children's play money. They spontaneously scatter Japanese phrases throughout their conversation; you mutter "Honda Civic" out of context and feel like a jerk.

So we went to Japan, had the best time of our lives, and returned home with enough memories and phrases to intimidate the few remaining citizens of Richmond who had yet to visit Japan. In the process, we learned that a little experience can be dangerous.

The Japanese language, for instance, is hard to speak and harder to understand. Martha does both, so she laughed at our feeble attempts to communicate. Had I, as Martha said, really invited two of her friends to lunch in the bathroom? Did Nancy, as a result of putting emphasis on a wrong syllable, address one of Martha's friends as a "train station"?

So we spoke only our native tongue, deciding to let our Japanese acquaintances figure out what we were saying. Even though most of them spoke no English, we talked loudly because everyone knows it helps if you shout. We simplified our English, too, which made us sound like natives in a bad jungle movie: "We are very hungry." "That is a pretty shoe." "Your umbrella is in my eye."

Their English is not perfect, either. One detour sign that was in both languages said: "Danger. Drive Sideways." The airline steward told us to avoid a certain hotel: "This hotel is a sort of rest house for an instant couple." And I heard (or imagined) one man muttering, "Chevrolet Coupe."

Eating in Japan is not a problem. There is a McDonald's on every fourth corner, as well as many Dairy Queen, Kentucky Fried Chicken, and Dunkin' Donuts restaurants. Eating there is a problem, however, if you have a daughter who insists you eat sushi (translation: raw fish). Japanese food is always served in an aesthetically pleasing way and with enormous courtesy. Psychologically, however, raw fish caused a dilemma for this provincial Hoosier who is used to charcoal broiling meat to near-incineration.

Raw fish is, well, raw. I wanted to please Martha. I wanted to be able to return home and mention we'd been to a sushi restaurant, and I didn't want to offend the Japanese nation. But I couldn't eat raw fish. Refusing to eat was embarrassing, but I still think it was better than throwing up my dinner.

There is more to tell, but the last thing you want to hear is a detailed account of somebody else's safari. Suffice it to say that our bilingual daughter-guide spared us from causing any major international incidents. And we learned that travel increases understanding. It broadens horizons and builds friendships.

Martha not only loves her Japanese husband, she loves her Japanese friends and her second country. When we watched a television show about confining Japanese Americans to stockades during World War II, she wept openly and said, "How could we do that?" Our visit recalled words from the old hymn, "In Christ there is no East nor West," and we now better understand the truth of its insight.

Martha's husband, Hideki, has parents who speak no English. When they came to Richmond for the wedding of their son, they experienced cultural shock. They tried a few English phrases that sounded funny to us and talked very loudly. And they thought we overcooked our food.

We understand, however, that they had a wonderful time and sometimes speak to their friends about Gropp's Famous Fish Restaurant in Syracuse, Indiana. They also salt their conversation with American phrases like "you guessed'er, Chester!" Their friends, we're told, are impressed and want to visit America.

I hope they do. Innocents who go abroad build love, respect, and appreciation for others. They can become like brothers and sisters and maybe doing so will help us avoid war and conflict. In the meantime, we can do one thing for our bilingual children—provide them with unlimited amusement as we butcher languages. Loudly.

9

A Contented New Year

Middle-aged, teetotaling Quaker diabetics usually stay home on New Year's Eve. Their children have grown up and left, so they no longer feel obligated to host "watch night" parties for the youth group, most of whom didn't attend because they were baby-sitting for parents who went to parties.

Staying home on New Year's Eve is not a practice shared by all middle-aged folks. It may, in fact, be an exception to a rule. Those of us who sit quietly in front of the television, sipping sugar-free beverages and munching popcorn (without butter), learn that thousands of people our age behave as if they were younger. And more virile.

Masses of people in large cities crowd together to watch a large luminous ball come tumbling down precisely at midnight. They yell "Happy New Year" into every available ear and hop up and down with enthusiasm—or to shake off the initial effects of frostbite. This is regarded as hilarious fun, particularly if you enjoy being smashed in the ribs and inhaling whiskey breath from inebriated neighbors. Rumor has it, in fact, that the Times Square midnight jamboree is really a planned event, jointly sponsored by the liquor industry and the Professional Pickpocket Association of New York.

Television then turns its attention to the nightclub scene on both coasts, and middle-aged viewers are able to watch their counterparts stagger about a ballroom as if they were dancing. Wearing funny-looking paper hats, men seize every opportunity to kiss someone else's wife, and the wives who get kissed respond with a degree of enthusiasm normally reserved for visiting the dentist.

The question, gentle readers, is this: Are we middle-aged folks who are sprawled on the couch holding hands with our spouses missing something? Even if we could afford to celebrate New Year's Eve in an expensive nightclub, would we enjoy it?

H. L. Mencken said that a Puritan, by definition, is a person who is terrified that somebody somewhere is having a good time. However, we are confident that merriment is not outlawed by God, and celebrating New Year's Eve is as good an excuse for a party as Thanksgiving is for eating turkey. This Puritan can confess, furthermore, that in his younger years he occasionally went dancing. (Note: I was brought up to believe that dancing was a sin. Nancy, brought up differently, persuaded me to dance. After dancing with me, however, she concluded that the way I did it *was* a sin.)

Anyway, why do we watch the desperate gaiety of New Year's Eve revelers and rejoice in knowing that we're not among them? Why is a calm, quiet, unexciting style of honoring New Year's Eve perfectly satisfying to us? True, we kissed each other squarely on the lips at the stroke of midnight, and my blood sugar rose slightly as a result. But would a perceptive psychologist conclude that subconsciously we're really jealous of those nightclubbers on the screen? Deep down inside, do we long to be young again?

Perhaps we never know for sure all our sinister motives, but the sight of grown men and women laboring mightily to create a hangover does little to inspire jealousy. A seemingly quiet manner of celebrating holidays may have something to do with age, but I doubt it. Age doesn't really matter—unless you're made of cheese—and growing older is not so bad when we consider the alternative.

It has to do with contentment. Feeling comfortable with one's spouse is a blessing far superior to any contrived pleasure, and looking forward to the years ahead brings anticipation, not resignation. As other well-blessed couples can affirm, love is blind and marriage is an eye-opener—but happily married people like what they see.

The key ingredient in this blessing is captured by the words of Antoine de Saint-Exupéry:

> Love does not consist in gazing at each other but
> in looking outward in the same direction.

If we share values and faith and maybe the common pleasure of doing unexciting things together, we'll enjoy New Year's Eve at home just fine. And the next day as well. And the day after that. And all the days we spend looking outward in the same direction.

Have a contented New Year.

10
WHEN PARENTS BECOME GRAND

When your grown children are happily married, it is reasonable to want grandchildren. Wise parents, of course, know better than to overtly pressure their children to have babies. They are careful never to mention the countless sacrifices they have made on behalf of their children without expecting any reward whatsoever except possibly a small grandchild.

Instead, the fathers of happily married children hint, suggest, and intimate that it would be nice to have something crawling under the Christmas tree next year. Happily married children learn to change the subject or deflect the hints. Or they purchase a puppy and refer to it as the "granddog."

As years go by, the pressure mounts. Comments about friends who are grandparents become more frequent. Pictures of Aunt Mary's grandchildren are left on the coffee table, and articles about trust funds for college education appear in the mail.

Your adult children, by now, ignore all hints and look heavenward with pained expressions. Or they invite small children from the neighborhood over to spill Kool-Aid on the rug when would-be grandparents are present.

Time, however, is on the side of the WBGs (would-be grandparents), and eventually God intervenes and their happily married children become pregnant. WBGs immediately go out and buy stuffed animals and forty rolls of film. All their personal plans are modified to honor the little creature whose coming will upgrade their status from in-laws to grandparents.

At this point the dialogue between the ATBGs (about-to-be-grandparents) and the ATBPs (about-to-be-parents) enters a new phase. ATB grandmothers become veritable fountains of advice about births. Surprisingly, ATB mothers seem interested and pay attention. ATB grandfathers lobby to have a boy baby named after themselves.

"Thomas James Northrop has a solid sound to it, don't you think?" he remarks casually after just having treated his son-in-law to a banana split at the Dairy Queen.

"We're thinking of calling a boy Alec," replies the ATBF.

"But no one in our family on either side has ever been named Alec," replies the ATBG with a snort that sounds like a gurgle.

"Exactly," responds the son-in-law, wiping from his upper lip the remnants of the banana split that his kind, generous, gracious, loving father-in-law purchased without any hidden motives whatsoever.

Undaunted, the ATBG works on his daughter who, by now, is only a few weeks from delivery and, theoretically, is vulnerable to suggestions and possibly intimidation. "I could happily set up a trust fund for a grandchild named Thomas James," the ATBG remarks, "or certainly remember him in my will."

The daughter, who has shared with her mother total control over her father for many years, rejects the offer outright. "I know what you're worth, Dad. It's no threat." Thus endeth the conversation.

When delivery day arrives, the issues change. Young married couples having babies approach the event differently from previous generations. They go to natural childbirth classes together and learn to breathe in rhythm and make funny sounds in unison. Husbands and their pregnant wives lie on the floor together and learn stuff about giving birth that their parents didn't even know enough about to ask questions.

Disposable diapers, which earlier generations thought represented a scientific advance, are outlawed because "They're not biodegradable." Pregnant women avoid all microwave ovens because of potential danger to the baby. (We had no microwave ovens to avoid!) Any baby clothes are selected with as much concern for style as function. Do diapers have style?

The huge difference is the way fathers now share in the delivery process. In an earlier time, an expectant father was isolated in a small room to wait by the hour until a doctor strolled out to tell him what kind of baby his wife had delivered. Now the father assists in the delivery process and sees his child before the mother does.

A new grandfather, however, continues to be isolated in a room to worry until someone comes out to tell him he's the father of a mother who had a son. New grandmothers, who know what's going on in there, smile with tiny tears in their eyes.

When it happens, finally, all past negotiations are null and void. New grandparents don't care if the baby is male or female, as long as it's healthy. The grandfather rejoices whether his grandson is named Alec or Rin Tin Tin, as long as he has fingers and toes and not paws.

Becoming a grandparent is to relive one of God's greatest miracles. Vicarious pain and vicarious joy are experienced. Continuing the generations, about which the Bible makes a big deal, is freshly understood. Scripture is fulfilled: "For to us a child is born, to us a son is given . . ." (Isaiah 9:6). And he is wonderful and mighty and ours!

Psychologists tell us that children born into extended families do well. When they have access to parents *and* grandparents *and* aunts *and* uncles *and* a community of supportive friends, they thrive. Those many smiling adults who buy huge teddy bears, snap pictures by the score, and stand in line to hold the little person benefit the child. Those babies need grandparents, and the grandparents, in turn, are free to behave foolishly and renew their hopes for the future of civilization. God's plan continues to work.

Historical note: On August 19, 1989, Charles Thomas Northrop was born to Sarah and Charles Thomas Northrop. His parents call him Chad. The maternal grandfather prefers his middle name.

11
SHIFTING THE TASSEL

She was slim and pretty and graduating with honors. "Thank goodness she looks like her mother," I said to myself as she crossed the stage to receive her diploma. Because I'm a faculty member, I was allowed to hand her that expensive piece of paper and, right there in front of everyone, give her a hug.

Ruth is the youngest of our four children. When she shifted the tassel, it meant she was leaving home. For most young people that moment comes earlier, after high school or because of the first job. Ruth, however, chose to go across the street to Earlham College where I teach. Leaving home had been delayed.

We had celebrated the graduation of her older sisters from college, and they, too, looked like their mother and were honor students. But Ruth's graduation was different. She was our baby. When the others left home,

I still had Ruth to tease and enjoy. And she had us to worry.

Where had the years gone? Children grow out of childhood, but parents never quite grow out of parenthood. It's like a biological miracle. The umbilical cord gets cut, but it stays connected to the parent.

As she walked across the stage, teetering on her high heels and clinging to her mortarboard for balance, memories flooded my mind.

She needed me a lot when she was little. Because she was the youngest, we didn't rush her through childhood. By the time Ruth came along, Nancy and I were professional parents.

When her sisters were toilet-trained, we thrilled to hear a toilet flush. With Ruth, the flush had lost its thrill.

Once, when she was eight, she fell off her bike and had to have eight stitches in her chin. She didn't cry even when the doctor sewed her up. I did, when she wasn't looking.

In junior high Ruth became a softball fanatic. She delighted in throwing a ball harder than most boys her age. Her games were invariably scheduled on nights hardest for me to attend, but I got there almost every time—and she always knew exactly when. In her final game, she made four hits—and three errors at shortstop. Parents win some and lose some, too.

In high school she tried to outdo her sisters. They had lots of stuff under their pictures in the yearbook, and

Ruth wanted more. So she played the flute and learned Spanish and wrote for the school newspaper. She needed me to haul her places, and it was clear that if I had had a uniform, a little cap, and a chauffeur's license, I would have been the perfect father.

She needed me to teach her how to drive a car with a stick shift. I grumbled about the cost of a prom dress she would wear only once. To teenagers a father is a banker provided by nature.

As a college student, Ruth didn't need me much, but every once in a while I had my uses. She often asked my advice about term papers and, once, about men. She took my advice about term papers.

During her college years, Ruth lived in a dormitory on campus or in Spain while on foreign study or in North Carolina on a summer job. But she lived at home her senior year because the dorm was too noisy. That clouded the fact that she was, as the baccalaureate speaker had said, "about to go into the world and the future would be in her hands."

I handed her the diploma, gave her a hug, and watched as she smiled all the way back to her seat. My throat was tight, but Ruth was relaxed and savoring the moment.

Doesn't Ruth know how tough the world is? She's ready to conquer it, but the world has a way of counterattacking. She's going to set it on fire, but what if her matches are wet? She won a scholarship to Columbia University to become a journalist. That means she'll be living in New York City, which is larger than Richmond, Indiana, and far more dangerous. As a journalism student, I'm told, she'll ride in police cars and become an aggressive, analytical reporter! My little girl who used to sleep with a night-light was entering the world for sure, and her future was certainly no longer in my hands.

It takes a while to accept the fact that we had run out of little kids whose hands we need to hold. Twenty-five years ago I was convinced we had a lifetime supply. We thought we would spend the rest of our lives tying their shoes or waiting up for them at night.

Progress for parents is measured in terms of things we no longer have to do for our children. Ruth's graduation meant the "to do" list had become so short we had no need for a list.

It was a moment of truth. The whole purpose of parenting is to help children achieve independence. And they do. But the cord stays connected, even though a parent's good-bye is a daughter's hello to the world.

So, world, welcome the last of our brood. You're not famous for being fair or even just. And, world, you can be cruel. But know this: She's not afraid of you and she speaks Portuguese and Spanish and writes English exceedingly well. In whatever language she expresses it, she knows she's not alone. Her parents are still connected to her and so is God.

Vaya con Dios, Ruth. You're ready.

12

SIBLING REVELRY

On April 7, 1991, my only brother, Frank, turned sixty. He is three and a half years older than I am, always has been, and when we were siblings at home, he took the edification of his younger brother seriously.

Frank provided an excellent moral example for me to follow, and he did well in school. He had my interests at heart, and I knew that if I lied, stole, or cheated, he would tell our parents or a teacher or whoever would be creative in punishing me. It was for my own good, he said.

Frank let me join a club of neighborhood children he had formed, even though I was younger than any other member. He let me pay the same dues as the others. Looking back, I can see why he eventually became Director of Development for Yale Divinity School.

When I was seven and he ten, we had an altercation.

Being larger than I was, he grabbed my toy gun and threw it into the furnace. Looking back, he claims he did so because he was clairvoyant and knew I would one day become a Quaker and renounce guns altogether.

During high school we worked side by side cutting weeds by hand from our parents' twelve acres of strawberries. I was better at cutting weeds than he, so I would hoe my row and much of his because he was a great storyteller and I wanted to stay close by and not miss anything. He knew exactly what he was doing. He was a Tom Sawyer named Frank.

We went to different colleges because he was a campus leader at Wabash College, and I didn't want to be the little brother all over again. Also, Wabash enrolled men only, and I wanted to go to a college where I could share academic life with women and possibly hug and kiss them.

In other respects, our paths have been similar. I followed him to Yale Divinity School, moving into the room in Seabury Hall which he'd vacated upon his graduation. In fact, he sold me his furniture, at a small profit, I learned later. He became a pastor, a YMCA executive, and now is Director of Development for Yale. I became a pastor, a teacher, and a seminary dean who had to raise money for a capital campaign.

We disagree about several matters—politics and certain fine points of theology. He's wrong, that's obvious, but I'm patient and expect to convert him to right thinking before one of us dies.

Frank demonstrates obsessive behavior in many ways. He gives attention to details that I would fail to notice if they were not pointed out to me—which he often does. He calls late at night, either interrupting our sleep or other activities married people do in bed, such as converse. He adores our children, possibly because he and his late wife had none of their own. They adore him in return, even though they, too, recognize the inadequacy of his political beliefs.

Frank, brought up properly in a small, Indiana town, should be more provincial than he is. Instead, he's traveled to every continent, including Antarctica. He became a bona fide New Yorker and regards it as the center of the universe. He boasts of its cultural advantages and one year attended over forty Broadway and off-Broadway plays. He delights even in the excesses of big city life. "New York garbage worker strikes are the biggest in the United States," he claims, arguing that such excesses breed creativity among the citizenry. During one garbage strike, for example, he gift wrapped two boxes of trash and left them in plain view in his car, knowing they would eventually be stolen!

Now Frank is sixty years old. I'm just enough younger to claim membership in the union of middle-agers. At sixty, Frank no longer can. He's, well . . . old. He gets discounts because of his age, and he takes advantage of every one. He talks more about estate planning than most young people do, although they should. Whenever he goes on one of his trips, he sends me a letter with instructions on what we should do if his plane crashes. His concerns about his estate are never morbid, but they are real.

He's probably going to leave his worldly goods to charities rather than to me or my children. This makes it easy to hope he lives many more years and enjoys many more trips to exotic places. It's important, however, that his younger and wiser brother use Frank's sixtieth birthday as an occasion to send a message.

Frank's legacy has already been given and received. In spite of his sophisticated life-style, he's pretty much the same person he has always been. We need to tell our brothers—and sisters, parents, children, and neighbors—that they're gifts to us from God. Just as they are.

Yes, they're imperfect, and I plan to continue helping my brother become aware of his imperfections. After all, he's a widower and has no wife to do it for him. By the time you've lived sixty years, an interested brother looking on can make a general evaluation.

Frank's one of the most generous people I know, even though his Christmas gifts are frequently bizarre. He's morally upright, and yet he continually helps people whose behavior he does not approve. The lists his obsessive personality makes are never-ending, but on them are the names of elderly and lonely people most others have forgotten.

So, happy birthday, Frank! You really shouldn't have burned my toy gun in the furnace, and please don't telephone after 10:00 P.M. You're forgiven, and thank God you've lived to be sixty, and I am able to tell you that you are loved and cherished. You know my words are sincere, and writing them is cheaper than a present.

PART III

INSIGHTS

When we're young, we are not expected to be wise, even though we think we are. Experience is still the best teacher, and it comes with the passing of time. In short, middle-aged Christian people ought to connect their faith to their lives better than when they were younger.

Life provides an unending supply of teachable moments. When one is stranded in an airport for eighteen hours because of fog, the ways people react show both sin and grace. We become observers of the passing—rather, stranded—parade.

The world is full of hostility at many levels, and middle-aged Christians will inevitably confront their share, usually without warning. Driving in heavy traffic on hot days through congested cities almost guarantees a challenge to our peacekeeping principles.

Adopting a son when he was two and helping him

blend into a family with three sisters, all of whom came from their mother's womb, was an adventure. The adoption was finalized when we were young, and Brett left home when we were middle-aged. The aging process was accelerated by the adoption, no doubt, particularly when his quest to find his "real mother" became apparent.

The sexual revolution in America gained momentum in the sixties and seventies. It's still going pell-mell. In contrast, our own romance and sexual attitudes seem outdated and provincial. Then why do we seem happier than all those celebrities who wallow in their libidos?

The test of time provides some important questions when you've been married over thirty years. A big one for Nancy and me has been equality. We both believe that men and women are equal partners and that God intended it so. We concluded, however, that inequality, freely chosen, is also a gift from God.

Teaching in a college long enough to earn a sabbatical leave is a luxury that would cause the most work-obsessed person to covet. A sabbatical is Bible-based, and using one as a time for "ripening" can be a source of spiritual refreshment.

Becoming a little older if we also become a little wiser is a fair trade-off in middle age. Insights about life don't come to us on a platter, neatly wrapped and perfectly timed. They come from experience, usually when we're busy doing something else.

13
A Clear View in the Fog

The situation: Dense fog blankets the area. Drivers of automobiles can still discern their hands in front of their faces, but this is little help in seeing the road. Airplanes are not flying, as all flights coming in and going out have been canceled.

The problem: A middle-aged teacher is supposed to fly to Wichita, Kansas, to give a speech to faculty and students of a small, church-related liberal arts college. The fog is not impressed. He and hundreds of others are grounded indefinitely with little hope of flying for at least eighteen hours.

The reactions: (1) The teacher calls the college and explains the situation. He asks: Can the speech be rescheduled to a later time? The college officials take the request under advisement. The teacher keeps making new reservations on later flights which continue being canceled approximately one hour after they are made. He resists the urge to suck his thumb and curl up in the prenatal position. (2) Other travelers respond in their own ways. Some become angry and abuse airline officials, particularly those responsible for the fog. One red-faced man is especially assertive: "Don't you understand? I *must* get to Boston *tonight!*" Also overheard are mumbled references to Mafia connections of airline officials and evaluations of their mental capacities as compared to an orangutan.

A few stranded travelers seem pleased and happy to be delayed. Most in this category are businesspeople on generous expense accounts who are set free to dawdle on company time with a clear conscience. Other happy strandees are those who now will not have time to visit their in-laws after all.

Several would-be travelers are neither angry nor happy. They wear looks of firm resignation not unlike those observed in the waiting rooms of dentists. Parents with small children are in this category, particularly those whose sons and daughters have begun to experience "sibling rivalry"—a fancy name for yelling, crying, and throwing popcorn at one another. Those heading for vacation sites also wear the look, and they can be identified by the absentminded manner in which they fondle their "Delta is ready when you are" buttons.

Further developments: (1) The school gets a last-minute substitute to give the speech this teacher was supposed to give. The substitute makes an outstanding presentation. The middle-aged teacher's speech remains in coat pocket where rust and mildew cannot reach it. It survives to be used another time. No outbreaks of decadence or attempts at suicide are reported because his speech was not delivered. (2) Anger and hostility had no effect on the fog. The man who had to get to Boston that night didn't, and Boston carried on without him. The siblings finally tired of their rivalry, a change in attitude encouraged by bribes, love, and threats of physical harm. Vacationers eventually got on planes that would take them where they wanted to go, which made them happy. Those who finally had to go places they would just as soon avoid took over responsibility for projecting gloom.

Religious insights: (1) Technology is a gift from God, but every so often fog reminds us it itself is not God. (2) The fog rolls over the just and unjust alike, and one's *attitude* toward it will determine who's ahead in the human race. Middle-aged people ought to be better than they once were in learning this lesson. By now, if no other lesson has been learned, knowing the world can function without us has been learned. The prayer that Alcoholics Anonymous uses at every meeting fits the middle-age experience:

> God, grant me the courage to change those things that must be changed, the serenity to accept those things that can't be changed, and the wisdom to know the difference.

(3) In spite of our missed appointments, canceled plans, and interrupted schedules, life goes on without us—sometimes even better. This provides an excellent lesson in humility, and sometimes it takes a heavy fog to make it clear.

14
HIGHWAY HATE

My trip to Marietta, Ohio, took me on Route 70 through the heart of Columbus. It was mid-June, and a hot, humid summer had a head start. Naturally, road construction was in full sway in downtown Columbus, and four lanes of traffic had been reduced to two by concrete barriers and sweaty men in orange hard hats.

Traffic was bumper-to-bumper. We stopped and started every few minutes, and I was trapped in the wrong lane. It was clearly marked: EXIT ONLY. If I stayed in that lane, I would either be treated to a side trip in and around southwest Columbus or possibly never heard from again. It was a dilemma.

We inched along. Within one hundred feet of the exit I was about to be forced to take, an opening in the lane to my left appeared in front of an enormous eighteen-wheeler. Because small Japanese cars can move faster than big trucks with slow acceleration, I eased into the other lane, breathing a small prayer of relief.

The prayer was premature. My switch of lanes had somehow infuriated the truck driver, and he roared up behind me with air horn blasting. A few hundred feet farther, the road widened to three lanes, and he pulled alongside me. Because we were temporarily stopped side by side, he slid over to the passenger side of his cab and launched a diatribe of words. He made a number of uncomplimentary references to my family tree. His torrent of words questioned my intellectual capacity and provided me with clear directions as to where I was going to spend eternity. He also suggested that I perform certain anatomical contortions that my middle-aged body was clearly unable to achieve.

Mercifully, traffic began to move again, so he concluded his oration, spat down on my windshield, and made a gesture that I'm confident had no religious meaning. During this time span, a sixty-second period that seemed years longer, I made no rebuttal of any kind. I wasn't sure what had triggered his anger, but "Have a nice day!" somehow didn't fit.

To be honest, I was frightened. My small Mazda was no match for his enormous truck, and his similarity to Godzilla was not totally a product of my imagination. In fact, Godzilla was friendlier. I know that I was glad when we finally cleared the construction zone, and my small car could run away.

I have reflected upon that experience many times.

Most of us have similar tales to tell, as the highway often provides a location for suppressed anger, indeed rage, to break loose. I am convinced that the truck driver would have punched me out had we been standing toe-to-toe on the street.

Such an incident reminds us how the Christian faith does not always provide instant answers to immediate problems. Understanding his circumstances might have helped, and Christians are well-advised to do so in matters of conflict. Had I walked a mile in his shoes, more accurately, driven five hundred miles in his truck, I might have been able to comprehend why his rage was so disproportionate to the event. Maybe his wife had left him for a Mazda dealer that morning. Perhaps several small cars had already cut in front of him, and my doing so was the final blow to his patience.

Any number of explanations might be correct, but they're irrelevant. In the moment of confrontation, we only have time to react, not analyze. I was both surprised and frightened. We Quakers are supposed to be peacemakers, indeed, all Christians are. My main interest on that day was to avoid war, and making no response was probably best. Not knowing what to say or do, however, was my reason for simply absorbing his abuse. A soft answer may, in fact, turneth away wrath, but I simply couldn't think of any answer, soft or hard.

The experience, however, is instructive. We learn a lot about ourselves and other people when we discover what makes us—or them—mad. We sometimes learn our moral significance by the things that, as the King James Version might put it, "ticketh us off."

People who usually rage at their children when milk gets spilled or garbage fails to be carried out had better examine their view of parenthood. Is a parent entitled to rage at the creatures who were gifts from God? Would the parent who abused a son or daughter be able to say that child was God's gift?

Spouse abuse is usually not simply an instantaneous reaction to an irritation. It comes out of a mind-set that says one spouse, almost always the husband, has both the right and the power to dominate the other.

When it was learned months after the fact that thousands of Panamanian civilians were killed or injured when we invaded their country in order to capture and punish Mañuel Noriega, some of our national leaders were embarrassed and sorry. Others continued to think our frustration and rage toward Noriega justified those deaths.

Jesus became angry a number of times. Once, He yelled at a fig tree because it didn't bear fruit. That turned out to be a parable with a deeper meaning. The people who angered Him, however, were money changers who were corrupting the faith community, or they were Pharisees who resented His healing on the Sabbath. Or He rebuked His own disciples when they tried to send the children away.

When we reach middle age, we will have had plenty of opportunities to learn from our anger. Anger in itself is not always wrong. Our rage toward others can be righteous anger, and sometimes raging at city hall is a call from God. But if all those sermons, Sunday school classes, Bible study groups, and mealtime conversations about right and wrong have done any good, we ought, in middle age, to get angry only for good reasons and in appropriate ways.

I don't know whether that truck driver was a church-going Christian. Based on our encounter, he demonstrated familiarity with religious language, but other evidence of faithfulness was missing. Had there been opportunity, I hope I would have been able to apologize for whatever driving sin I had committed. In ongoing relationships where there is a possibility of repentance, confession, forgiveness, and healing, awful acts of rage can be addressed.

The Peaceable Kingdom has not yet been established, however, so we continue to live in the in-between times—like now. We can learn from our conflicts, and live in that faith and power that takes away the occasion for rage.

And sometimes, we simply must not switch lanes on hot days during roadway construction. I know I never will again.

15

ADOPTING AND ADAPTING

Brett paced the front porch like an expectant father trapped in a box. He was dressed in his Sunday best, even though it was a weekday. He had come home immediately after school, not his usual practice. He had shaved, dressed, and begun his nervous pacing two hours before his 5:00 P.M. appointment.

Our adopted son was meeting his birth mother that day. He had not seen her since infancy, which meant he knew her virtually not at all. Brett was seventeen years old.

His interest in his biological roots had been present for several years. He had often asked us questions about who his mother was, and at one point we had contacted the county welfare department that had handled the process. In our state, such information is not available until the adoptee is at least eighteen; under certain circumstances, it's never available.

Undeterred, Brett had examined microfilms of the local paper's birth announcements for several days on and about April 13, 1964. He searched for clues to his own identity, but in those days, births to unwed mothers were announced under a cloud of ambiguity.

He might never have found out had it not been for the unusual Christmas card that arrived at my office a few days before the holiday. The card had a return street address and a zip code but no name, initials, city, or state on the envelope. The postmark indicated it had been sent from Vero Beach, Florida.

Inside was a traditional Christmas card and a two-sentence message, unsigned. "Scarcely a day passes in which I don't think of the baby I gave up. Thank you for giving him love and a good home."

Why this message after so many years without contact? How did she know who had adopted Brett since he had been in foster care for a year before we became involved? Given the incomplete address, did she want to contact Brett or not? We knew Brett wanted someday to meet his birth mother. Nancy and I weren't sure we did, but it seemed right to try.

So we sent a letter to "occupant" at the address stated on the envelope and took a chance that Vero Beach was the city that matched the address. Our letter said that we were glad she continued to cherish Brett and that he had often wondered about his birth mother. We gave her our phone number and invited her to call if she wished.

The reason it seemed to be the right thing to do is that the literature about adoption had helped us intellectually understand the dynamics of the experience. The literature explained that most adopted children long to know who their birth mothers are. We also learned that biological mothers feel enormous ambivalence, often years after having given a child away. And we had suddenly been forced to examine how adoptive parents feel about a sudden invasion into a longtime relationship.

The Art of Adoption (Acropolis Books, 1976), a book by Linda Cannon Bergess, was persuasive. She warned against adoptive parents protecting their own needs by ignoring their child's biological mother. She wrote,

> While they presume rejection by their biological parents, adoptees nevertheless identify with them. The sense of unworthiness which results may inhibit their growth, keeping them dependent and immature, abnormally grateful to their adopters and guilty in thoughts of disloyalty toward them.

Our heads were persuaded. Our hearts, however, were not so sure. Most adoptive parents will recognize our feelings. Yes, we wanted to do the right thing for our son, particularly since his teenage years had demonstrated considerable rebellion and he was not always sure he had been dealt a good hand. But, darn it, we had invested ourselves in this boy, loving him through thick and thin. By age seventeen, there had been lots of thin.

Where had this woman in whom he had such a deep interest been all this time? Nancy had cleaned and sterilized his room every day of a two-year period while he outgrew a bronchial condition, not this woman. Nor had she been the one who met with the vice-principal (the one in charge of vice) when Brett had gotten into massive trouble in school.

Our thoughts, particularly Nancy's, were similar to what another adoptive parent had responded to her six-year-old's question, "What was my real mother like?" That woman had said, "Your real mother is the one who brings you up, who takes care of you, and sees you're well and happy." Obviously, she had answered her own question, not what the child had asked. We understood.

A few days later, Leah called. Brett's birth mother had received our letter and, when she got the courage, called our home. Leah was weeping on the phone, and it was clear that Brett was not the only one who longed to see, hear, and touch another once connected by an umbilical cord.

We laid plans. She was coming to Richmond in a few months to visit relatives, the ones who had provided her with news clippings about Brett's adventures in 4-H, church, and junior high basketball. We invited her for dinner at 5:00 P.M. on a warm spring evening.

Leah arrived at exactly 5:00 P.M. Brett ran down the porch steps to the sidewalk in front of our house and stopped. Leah got out of the car, and stopped. They stared, smiling and crying at the same time. They embraced and said things we couldn't hear. We were watching from the front window. We cried, too. Hollywood could not have arranged a more poignant scene.

That moment is the best remembered one of their reconciliation. Leah was still a young woman. Pregnant with Brett at sixteen, she had married, two years later, a man who didn't want the bastard child, so she gave him up for adoption. She had two sons by her husband, and Brett suddenly had two half brothers. She was bright and pretty, and Brett proudly introduced her to his friends, our neighbors, his teachers, and even strangers they met on the street. Leah was gracious to us, happy for Brett, and expressed hopes of staying in touch after she returned to Florida.

Nancy was warm and understanding. She was a little hurt because Brett's joy in introducing Leah was far greater than he had demonstrated when Nancy had taken him for doctors' appointments. But her love for Brett was deeper than her hurt feelings. Our heads had been correct, for a change. We had done the right thing.

That day is nine years old at this writing. Brett managed to graduate from high school in the upper quarter of the bottom fiftieth of his class, mostly because Nancy stayed on his case every night for a month so he wouldn't flunk the courses he had to have to graduate. After graduating, he enrolled in a twelve-week course where he learned how to be a reservation clerk for an airline. The school was located in Florida, so he stayed with Leah for a few months after completion.

Now twenty-six, Brett has returned north and lives about four blocks from our home. He's buying a house, and we helped him make the down payment. He's really glad he discovered Leah, and his longing to know her has been fully satisfied. He keeps company with a fine young woman we like very much. They may one day get married.

We see him often, particularly when he's broke. His values and life-style are observedly different from our own, but he knows that Nancy is his real, not pretend, mother. Brett knows he's our son.

Middle age provides opportunity to reflect on outcomes of earlier key decisions. A Christian perspective enables us to respond to outcomes that are not always precisely what we might have wanted. We can rejoice and give thanks *in* all circumstances if not *for* all circumstances. Yesterday is experience. Tomorrow is hope. Today can be enough if we rejoice in what is rather than long for what didn't happen. Enough, after all, is a lot.

16
SEX IN THE SLOW LANE

Middle age is when we stop criticizing older generations and find fault with younger ones. This is not a new insight. Socrates said, "Children today are tyrants. They contradict their parents, gobble their food, and tyrannize their teachers." At least I think it was Socrates who said that. It may have been my father right after we took our children there for a visit.

Certainly there are attitudinal differences between generations. The question is: Are things better or worse?

Consider sex, for example. Sex has long been used to sell us stuff, but never so explicitly or continually as now. When I was a boy (Note: A sure sign of middle age is a sentence that begins, "When I was a boy. . . ."), before television, sex appeal was used in radio commercials. The voices of two small boys would come over the air waves, each saying, "My Daddy uses Crank Shave Cream." Then, a woman's voice, sultry and dripping innuendo, would ooze the words, "My da-dee uses Crank Shave Cream, too." I wasn't old enough to shave, but I knew Crank Shave Cream had more to do with sex than whiskers.

Television ads make that verbal come-on seem as innocent as fresh-fallen snow. Now the whole family becomes acquainted with "personal care" products that used to be purchased in drug stores in plain brown paper. Men and women advertise their underwear while posing in it. Young women, dressed in costumes so scanty we're never sure if they're inside trying to get out or outside trying to get in, sell us automobiles or cornflakes.

Television programs are frank, explicit, and full of colorful language. Topics such as sexual disease, spouse trading, and prostitution are discussed frequently on talk shows—often by veterans of the experience. Celebrities who have been married so often they use wash-and-wear wedding clothes offer marital advice. Living together and having babies without being married is commonplace. Soon the only way the *National Enquirer* will be able to shock us will be in an article about two virgins who get married after a long courtship and live happily ever after.

Such openness didn't happen overnight, of course. Those of us who have reached middle age have at least been spectators to the changes, often with our mouths hanging open. Having grown up in a family in which my grandmother hid the underwear inside the pillowcases when she hung the wash on the line, current sexual openness is like living on a different planet.

Have you been to the movies lately? If PG ratings mean "Parental Guidance" is suggested, Ma Barker and the Marquis de Sade must be the parents they had in mind. A movie that is awarded an R will feature nudity, obscene language, violence, and bedroom scenes in livid color.

Some of us, distressed by the sex and violence of most Hollywood productions, stopped going to the movies. We purchased VCRs so we could bring sex and violence into the home. Renting videotapes has become a growth industry in the United States, and small towns with only one service station and grocery store will offer movie cassettes of all kinds. We can rent both *Bambi* and *Debbie Does Dallas* right next to *Good Housekeeping* and Jeane Dixon's horoscopes. The irony is that many X-rated movie houses have closed because consenting adults can rent pornographic video cassettes easier and cheaper.

Criticizing a younger generation for this state of affairs helps clear the sinuses and increases the flow of blood to our cheeks and ears. It is not, however, fair. Middle-aged people are among the heaviest viewers of video cassettes and buyers of *Playboy* and *Playgirl*. Hugh Hefner, after all, is a middle-aged man who exploits the sexual fantasies of all ages.

So what's a concerned, reasonably moral, conscientious middle-aged Christian to do? If this author knew for sure, he wouldn't be writing books. He wouldn't have to, as people would pay him large sums of money after climbing up a mountain to seek his advice. We've learned that one of the best ways to sell X-rated books, movies, and cassettes is to oppose them openly. And some pictures of naked people are art while others are dirty.

Christ and culture have never been synonymous. Often—the present time included—they've been at odds. Certain evangelists have confused the issue by preaching against the sexual sins they were committing when the church service was over. Middle-aged Christians at least have perspective about sex that allows us to make decisions based on experience.

If God intended that sex be expressed in a context of fidelity and responsibility, we can decide what to see and what to avoid on a case-by-case basis. One movie will have a message worth hearing in spite of foul language or blush-bringing scenes. Another will be trash for its own sake, and we'll have to decide which is which. Parents and grandparents who can make such choices had better be able to articulate why and not just say no.

Our best role models for sexuality still come from the men and women in our own churches and neighborhoods. Celebrity status has no legitimacy for sexual role modeling. Otherwise, we could say to our children, "Be like Elizabeth Taylor," or, "Follow the example of Jack Nicholson." Being married for many years is a far more credible authority for sexual advice than being married many times.

Permissive and premature sex is glorified in our society because there is money to be made from doing so. Middle-aged people, even those whose hot flashes are lukewarm, buy into its values. And we should know better.

We won't know what sexual values are promoted in a movie until it's over. We dare not judge youth too harshly for the attitudes they have acquired. Our generation probably was repressed in terms of sexual attitudes. We have our own temptations, lusts, and mistakes to confess. Victims of sexual abuse, adultery, and betrayal are plentiful. Jesus forgave the woman caught in the very act of adultery and forgiveness for those who fall short is a key to Christ's gospel.

So, better than wringing our hands and chanting in unison, "O ain't it awful," we can be sexually faithful and try again and again to sort out the good stuff from the bad. Sex is here to stay, and so are we for a while longer. Can we show a sexually confused society a better way? If not we, who?

17
EQUAL MARRIAGE

When Nancy and I wed in 1957, we shared assumptions about marriage that were traditional. Not that we had talked about our respective roles as wife and husband very much beforehand; we simply took certain understandings for granted.

We were sexually attracted to each other, but we made it to our wedding night as virgins because of strict moral upbringing and, on my part, many laps around the track and occasional cold showers. Modern hedonists will not understand, but several of us middle-aged folk connected love to sex right from the start. Exploiting each other or dominating the other in a bedroom wasn't an option.

Looking back, we allow ourselves the arrogant thought that we practiced sexual equality better than Dr. Ruth could have imagined possible. Innocence and a lack of experience combined with a heap of desire and a high view of marriage can result in equality. We really could respect each other in the morning. And the afternoon. And the next day.

We had a traditional marriage in other ways. I expected to be the breadwinner, and she a homemaker. Because I was a pastor, there wasn't a lot of bread to win, and Nancy made it clear from the outset that the person who was going to pick up after me was me. Nevertheless, our roles were more or less defined.

In pastoral ministry, however, traditional roles are often blurred. When we lived next door to the church, committees, Sunday school classes, and discussion groups often met in our home. Couples came there for premarital counseling, some of which Nancy provided. The youth group and occasional strays from it preferred our home to their own. While it was clear that I was the pastor and she the spouse, the ministry is a vocation quite different from medicine, law, or business. In those professions, the breadwinner goes away in the morning and comes home in time for dinner in the evening. The pastoral ministry is often shared by both spouses. I've often wondered how celibate clergy manage.

We did not share food preparation and housekeeping equally. Nancy has prepared nearly all the meals during our thirty-three years together, and I've picked up most of the checks in restaurants. She's done more laundry, and I've mowed the grass more often than she. One has not been master and the other slave, but our roles have been more traditional than many modern couples could have tolerated. And I admit—nay, confess—I've had the better deal.

I did a lot of the child care when our three daughters and one son were growing up, but Nancy's presence made our home a reasonably orderly, happy place. Whenever I couldn't stand the clutter or the noise, I could leave to do "God's work." The work was important, but leaving was often a refreshing choice. In a traditional marriage, winning the bread has usually been an acceptable excuse for escaping the chaos or boredom of homemaking. Nancy, because of her role, couldn't escape so easily.

When we reach middle age and the children have left, we husbands who have had the better deal in a traditional marriage can own up to that fact. If we don't, our grown daughters who have a different definition of equality in marriage will yell at us. Therefore, I decided to discuss the issue with the woman who had promised to love me and wash my socks.

So, as we sat by the fire sipping the sugar-free hot chocolate Nancy had prepared, I confessed the nagging realization described above. Middle age, after all, is a good time for such confessions. I am allegedly wiser than I once was and, since the nest is empty, I can confess without having to change my ways.

She agreed that the breadwinner role has more esteem than the homemaker role. We had always shared a single bank account, but not having "her own" money wasn't the issue. The issue was the way money is equated with worthiness. Our society, such as it is, values wage earners more than it does spouses who stay at home, nurture the children, and do windows.

When Nancy was teaching school or working as a service representative for a telephone company, she felt more worthy than she did working just as hard at home. It's a point of view many middle-class, middle-aged women have received from our society. The fact that I, the man who had promised to love her and take out the garbage, regarded her as equal and worthy, employed or not, was irrelevant.

"How would you feel, Tom," she asked, "if you were always dependent on me for money?" I had been while in seminary, but we both knew that was temporary. I pondered that question while I fixed us both a second cup of sugar-free hot chocolate.

I realized I couldn't know how she felt because I had never been in her position. I recalled that she had made all the career adjustments in our life together. When I became dean of our seminary, Nancy stopped teaching so she would be free to host meetings in our home and travel with me to distant places. I remembered how she had been passionate in insisting that our three daughters should be equipped for a career, married or not.

"Don't misunderstand," said the woman who had promised to honor me and scrub my back. "I chose to have a traditional marriage and be at home with the kids. You've always taken me seriously, and I've not been left out of major decisions. But by the world's standards, A.D. 1991, I'm less important in a marriage than a breadwinner."

We sat in silence for a while. Quakers often do that when they're listening for the voice of God. Or when God has spoken through a woman and her husband doesn't know what to say.

She was right. Our marriage has always been the one constant, dependable, encouraging element of my life. Everything else had been flawed. My career had been modest, parenthood had had some sharp pains, and millions of people had never read one of my books.

Our marriage had been a blessing, but it had not been the model of equality I had rationalized it to be. Nancy had gone the second mile, denied herself, and adapted her life to mine and our children.

She broke the silence. "Don't misunderstand, man of my life. I know you adore me, and the kids love me, and I'm the only one the dog loves in the whole family. And you need me. I plan to outlive you, in fact, because you'd be a mess if I weren't here to look after you."

Then she kissed me squarely on the lips. And got up to do the dishes. There may not be such a thing as an equal marriage. A good marriage is like a firm handshake. There's no upper hand. The truth is, in a good marriage one partner adapts more than the other. My guess is that wives, more often than husbands, do the adapting. Sublimation is a jargon phrase from psychology. It means that some people find meaning and purpose in their lives by setting aside some of their dreams for the sake of other realities.

Those of us who benefit from the choice others make for our sake are among God's fortunate people. I wish society could value the homemaker role more than it does. Valuing breadwinners more is unjust. It's not fair. The system, however, shows no signs of changing.

But what this husband can do, at least, is celebrate the gift of love that became mine on September 1, 1957. It's a gift that keeps on giving until death do us part.

18
A TIME FOR RIPENING

Sabbatical leaves are gifts from God that are funded by the operating budget. Schools and colleges are way ahead of churches and other institutions that do not provide sabbaticals. This explains why there are so many more teachers than clergy.

The irony is that a sabbatical year has biblical roots and deep religious meaning. In Leviticus we learn that every seventh year loans were canceled, pledged property was restored, and land remained fallow. Whatever grew on the uncultivated land was left to poor people and strangers. (Historical note: The cancellation of debts was eventually circumvented through legal reforms instituted by a famous Pharisee, Hillel. In our day, conservative legislatures and trustees have similarly restricted such benefits, thereby establishing a connection between the Pharisees and the Republicans.)

As a seminary teacher-administrator who is embarking upon his first year-long sabbatical at age fifty-six, such information is important. Leaving one's post for an entire year suggests both opportunity and peril.

Anticipation runs high. It may be, in fact, the best part of the experience. For example, deans attend lots of meetings. And as one struggles through the fourth committee meeting called to decide where bulletin boards should be placed in a classroom building, questions about the "meaning of life" occur. Does God care where or whether bulletin boards are attached to walls?

Committees, often referred to as "standing" rather than "doing," can be tedious. The word *committee* is a noun signifying "many," but in the minds of most it means "not much." The writer of Ecclesiastes undoubtedly had just returned from a committee meeting when he said, "What has been will be again, what has been done will be done again; there is nothing new under the sun" (1:9).

Those of us with extroverted personalities and skinny bottoms are worn down by years of committees, task forces, strategic planning, and meetings for business. Frustration and fatigue blend and cause resentment toward those patient souls who feed upon meetings as if they were manna. And doing physical harm to other members of the committee, even the Baptist, is not an option. Nor is taking a nap in the prenatal position while sucking on a wet towel.

The *anticipation* of a whole year without such meetings rejuvenates! A whole year with no reports to make, consensus to sense, or administrative mistakes to correct. Heaven, thy name is sabbatical!

Sabbaticals also feature, usually, a *farewell event* in which you are honored for having survived six years of committees without hitting a Baptist. It is a public recognition that your LEAVE is near! Colleagues, students, and friends gather to say complimentary words and give you gifts. Such events may be the closest one ever comes to attending his own funeral.

The best friends you have in the world stand up and exaggerate all the good things you've done, conveniently overlooking the legion of mistakes and acts of stupidity you have perpetrated. They tease you, tell lies, and create the general impression that, without your efforts, the school would have closed and the building sold to the Veterans of Foreign Wars for a bowling alley. The farewell event, of course, is wonderful, and the most obvious conclusion is that the best part of the job is leaving it.

Soon, however, a touch of reality intrudes. It happens when we remember that all these people have come to celebrate your *departure*. The comment P. T. Barnum made when he was asked why hundreds of people attended the funeral of a thoroughly disliked, miserly grouch is sobering. He said: "Give people what they want and they'll turn out."

Reading the fine print in the definition of a sabbatical nurtures more realism. It is not a vacation. It is a time for "retooling." You are supposed to design a plan for your sabbatical. You're supposed to create a new course or transform an old one. Studying an ancient ruin is an option or doing research on an obscure scholar whose influence has been underestimated is another. Chances are your research will reveal why his influence was underestimated. It was deserved!

You also discover other existential realities. Because you're on sabbatical leave, your income is cut in half. The good news is that you won't have to poke around those ancient ruins after all because you can't afford the trip. The bad news is that you will be able to study poverty based on the personal experience of begging on street corners.

So what's a tired, needy ex-dean to do as he fluctuates between euphoria and reality? The answer is clear: I don't know. I tend to cling to the warm feelings of anticipation and the lingering warmth of the Farewell Event. Our savings are not yet depleted: most of the leave time is ahead of me. So, I bask in the hope that the religious meaning of sabbatical will be experienced.

The seventh year—the sabbatical—is a time for neither working nor fretting. Instead, it is a time for ripening, a time to labor, not work. As Lewis Hyde wrote in *The Gift* (Vintage, 1983):

> In ancient days a seventh part of a person's time was set aside for non-work. Nowadays when a teacher gets a sabbatical, he or she may try to

finish six years of unfinished chores. But first he should put up his feet and see what happens.

We either ripen, or we don't. Work is dictated by what has to be done. Labor, by contrast, has its own interior rhythm. "It sets its own pace," says Lewis Hyde, and "is usually accompanied by idleness, leisure, even sleep."

Thanks, friend, I needed that. I feel riper already.

PART IV
LEGACIES

We both receive and provide legacies. In middle age we discover what our parents have given us, and we also glimpse the values and customs our children claim from all we've offered for the taking. To know what you intended to be remembered for but to have lived long enough to see what was chosen is both sobering and comic.

Family rituals may be repeated by the next generation, but most often they get modified, nay, translated into something else. Watching this happen to my children and theirs reminds us that both virtues and sins are passed along.

Halloween for most American families has as much connection to the Christian faith as shaving soap does to electric razors. Even so, Halloween among some Christian groups has become potentially pleasing to God. Translating it into something better brings new meaning to a thoroughly corrupted holiday.

Grandbaby-sitting provides an up-close and personal opportunity to see what has been passed along through custom, if not chromosomes. And the main lesson grandparents who baby-sit learn is that they're substitutes for the varsity (the parents)—and that's a nice, not a jealous, feeling.

Those of us with grown children gain a perspective on a key question every conscientious Christian asks: Will they have faith? If the answer is yes, that's good news, but we learn their faith is not a regurgitated form of our own.

A gift middle-aged, long-married people nurtured for themselves is life in the Comfort Zone. Two people share a relationship that produces a weird kind of independence *and* bonding that Siamese twins might envy.

What most of us don't want to leave behind is a sense of rigidity, inflexibility, or "set-in-our-ways-ness." God often has plans for us late in life, and being ready to hear God's call keeps middle-aged Christians alert.

This section concludes with an essay about the death of my mother. Dying is the natural order. It is the way God arranged existence. Deaths that come out of order are harder to accept as a legacy. Yet, Christians can rejoice in a good death which usually is an extension of a good life. Mother lived a life of faith, temperance, and commitment to others. We mourned the separation her death caused, but, at fifty-four, I was old enough to see the legacy she left all of us, particularly her sons. Goodness can be passed along, and Mother's death reminded us that for Christians, death is a doorway to life.

19
TRADITIONS

Families, by definition, establish rituals. When our children were small, a nightly pattern of behavior was as predictable as the ending to the Twenty-third Psalm. It was the bedtime ritual, and both children and parents had parts to play. There was the bathroom routine in which children were to wash their faces, brush their teeth, and tend to lower anatomical needs. Sarah, Martha, Brett, and Ruth extended this ritual as long as they could. Our role was to wait until the proper moment to issue a hurry-up call. Usually, a strongly worded ultimatum that included the phrase "I mean it" was issued by a parent. Firm ultimatums provide excellent exercise for parental facial muscles and consistently promote giggling by the children.

Next in the bedtime ritual came the reading of the story. Choosing the story, of course, required considerable discussion as to selection and length. Whatever the final choice, there was little need to read it in its entirety as the children knew it by heart. Any effort by the parent to short-circuit the experience by skipping a few pages caused a child to rise up from the bed in righteous indignation: "Daddy, you promised to read the whole story!" Changing the ritual was not permitted, and wise parents learned to perform exactly as their children had trained them.

Other rituals marked our place, so to speak, in the growing-up years of our children. Most of them were internal to our family experience. Saturday morning breakfast at the Waffle House was one. My mother was usually included, and this meant our children were better behaved than usual. We even had "our" waitress, a pleasant woman who overlooked the inevitable smeared pancake syrup, knowing that our guilt feelings would inspire a generous tip.

Trips to the mall, while irregular, also followed established patterns. The older girls would disappear together, I would accompany Brett in order to protect him from physical harm by clerks he would pester, and Ruthie would lead her mother to every store that sold toys or food. We always agreed upon a meeting place and time, and at least twice over a five-year period everybody made it on schedule.

Holidays, too, are shaped by family traditions. Christmas Eve, for years, was reserved for being with my parents. On Christmas Day we went to Indianapolis to open presents with Nancy's family. When, finally, our home was the one to which people came to celebrate Christmas, we chose Christmas Eve as our family time. Each year we had a program that included unchanging elements. There was music. Sarah would play her violin, Martha the piano, Ruth the flute. Brett, after a fashion, sang. Having no musical talents, their parents listened. Nancy read the Christmas story from Luke, and I always read "The Gift of the Magi" by O. Henry. We'd read it every year since we'd been married, and it had become a tradition. A tradition is not simply what you have when you're too lazy to think up something new. It is a point of stability, something dependable and unchanging in a world that is neither.

We always opened presents beginning with the youngest child. Brett, next-to-youngest, had to wait until Ruthie opened her first present. She had never gotten caught up in the greed of the season, so her main delight was in delaying the process long enough to cause her brother serious psychological pain.

The present-giving ritual taught children the delight of making others happy by giving them gifts. Our children, to this day, compete less in terms of what they receive than they do in seeing whose gift will be the best liked. Because I was oldest, I opened my presents last, which meant that I had to wait to see what color the socks and underwear were going to be this year.

Nancy was, and is, the best person to whom to give gifts. She covets practically nothing, but she delights in whatever she's given. When the children were little, they gave her cheap perfume and cheaper earrings. Her delight was genuine, and she wore the perfume even though it smelled like disinfectant and the earrings until her ears turned green.

Family rituals show how we feel about ourselves and our loved ones. Middle age is a time when old patterns are changed and new rituals established. Healthy families only substitute, never eliminate, rituals. They enable us to see where we've been, where we are, and what will continue after we're gone.

The year my mother was terminally ill with cancer, we videotaped our Christmas Eve celebration. The program was better than usual. The children were adults. Sarah had given up the violin, and Brett's voice had changed for the better. The program featured a funny skit that spoofed our family tradition. Brett, twenty-four, couldn't wait to open his gifts. Ruth took her time, Martha made us laugh, and our sons-in-law wondered openly if they had married into a weird family. Sarah and Charlie announced that their child was on the way, so Jesus' birthday had special meaning.

Traditions get passed along but are modified in the process. It's like owning the ax Abraham Lincoln used to cut wood except that it has a new blade and a different handle. History connects family traditions.

Sarah and Charlie, on most Friday nights, eat at Pizza Hut because it has a good salad bar, and Chad can sit in a little chair and eat, squeeze, and spill his food without being cited by the health department. One waitress goes out of her way to serve them and admire Chad, obviously a woman of taste and breeding.

Martha and Hideki live in Japan, so we aren't familiar with their favorite sushi restaurant. Tokyo department stores put up a few plastic Santas, but Christian rituals are conspicuous by their absence. Yet, Martha and Hideki decorate a little tree, open presents, and play Christmas carols. We talk on the phone on Christmas day, really our Christmas Eve, given the fourteen-hour time difference. It's like, you know, a tradition.

Not long ago we baby-sat for Chad and put him to bed. He stalled the process as long as he could and insisted his grandmother read him a certain book he already knew by heart. Next year Martha and Hideki will modify their rituals somewhat because their baby will have arrived, crying probably in both English and Japanese. The beat goes on.

Those of us who have lived past fifty know that sins can be passed to later generations. The good news is that traditions also get passed along, often without fanfare, but usually with meaning. Rituals are a means of grace, and witnessing the transition is worth living long enough to observe. One of the great benefits of middle age is that we can be eyewitnesses to our own history. It's a reason to celebrate and give thanks, so long as we don't stay up too late.

20

TRICK OR TREAT IN THE NAME OF CHRIST

When Christmas decorations appear in stores and a visit from Santa Claus to a local shopping mall is imminent, we know Halloween is near at hand. Not that Halloween lacks its own identity. Come the end of October, any village with more than one child will be descended upon by small ghosts and their ghoul friends. Children not otherwise allowed to cross the street by themselves roam in packs. Armed with large sacks, they work both sides of the street with the traditional ultimatum: "Trick or treat, smell my feet, give me something good to eat." Witches, goblins, ghosts, hoboes, demons, skeletons, lions, tigers, and cowboys appear on doorsteps in such abundance that the competition for candy is a veritable zoo.

Whole communities organize for Halloween, adding extra police to direct traffic, establishing hours for the great shakedown to occur, and discouraging the citizenry from putting razor blades in apples. Local businesses feature trick-or-treat specials, and the children collect enough sweets to upset their stomachs, destroy their appetites, and substantially advance tooth decay.

Parents share in Halloween festivities, too. They chaperone groups of goblins as they systematically descend upon each house on their hit list. They deal with the child who inevitably will need to go to the bathroom and invariably will be dressed in a costume consisting of three layers of clothing, each of which is safety-pinned to the other. Parents also "help" carve faces on pumpkins, a creative chore that includes scooping out handfuls of innards, a task not unlike draining a septic tank.

To be seriously critical of Halloween, however, is unnecessary and possibly grounds for deportation. Nevertheless, the celebration of Halloween as it occurs in America in 1991 raises some sobering questions. We forget that two lesser-known holidays immediately follow Halloween and, in fact, originally gave it birth. One is All Saints' Day on November 1 and is observed in certain Roman and Anglican traditions. It is a day on which saints not otherwise mentioned by name on the calendar or who were historically anonymous are commemorated.

The other holy day, which follows on November 2, is All Souls' Day, an occasion observed with solemnity, usually including Requiem Masses. The day commemorates "holy souls" who have departed this life and are in the intermediate state, awaiting their final destination.

To most Christians, however, All Saints' Day and All

Souls' Day are virtually unknown. That Halloween once had sacred and serious connections comes as a complete surprise. Yet, a closer look reveals how an original intent—honoring the departed—evolved into a totally secular celebration. Over the years, we moved from Requiem Masses to masses of small children shouting "boo" at passersby. Horror movies on TV (*Halloween Part III*) easily outdraw services for Christian saints.

That evolution, in fact, may be the scariest part of Halloween. In spite of the many sermons about keeping Christmas Christian and against turning Easter into a bunny rabbit celebration, most of us don't really expect these celebrations to lose their sacred roots. Halloween is a sobering reminder that it can happen.

There is also a redemptive possibility. It reminds us that God is still running the universe and is not bound by our interpretations of holidays. The squeals of delight and excitement among children are surely pleasing to God. Furthermore, as children—often under the sponsorship of a local church—trick-or-treat for UNICEF, an important event happens. We see children rising above greed to work for others. They may learn more about compassion for the world's hungry and poor than they ever would have learned from remembering old souls and old saints.

In faith, we can affirm that God is Lord of the living and the dead, of Halloween and All Souls, of children with full stomachs and empty ones. If Halloween can remind us of this truth, it will be a holy day and not merely a holiday. Someday we might even hear, "Trick or treat in the name of Christ," and be glad.

21
GRANDBABY-SITTERS

Our first grandchild lives only two miles away. So do his parents, but that's incidental. Chad is master of his house and his grandparents' hearts.

Because of this easy proximity, we spend lots of time with him. His parents approve because they trust us, and we work cheap. So we frequently volunteer to keep an eye on him for an hour, which always means to keep two eyes on him for three hours. Doing so helps grandparents learn experientially why God decided young adults are the ones to have babies. People over fifty, when they care for an active toddler with more curiosity than a rocket scientist, are like old movies. They are gray, slow motioned, and often break in the middle.

Even so, baby-sitting for Chad is a labor of love. We are excellent evaluators of his progress. It is objectively true that Chad is a superior human being with outstanding chromosomes from his mother's side of the family. Lest you think we are biased, we have over two hundred candid snapshots of him and all the secretaries at the seminary agree, at least those still employed there.

Knowing that Chad is a rare specimen of humanity, however, increases grandparental responsibility. The nicest thing about a toddler is that everything he does is wonderful. Everything he does is also wearing, and small boys need to sleep so that baby-sitting grandparents can rest.

When the children of middle-aged people were small, the parents were younger. So when the first grandchild started taking over our lives, we examined our memory banks in order to cope. We dusted off Dr. Spock. We baby-proofed our home, putting all sharp instruments up high. We purchased plastic covers for electrical outlets. We even removed our coffee table with the sharp corners, as it was too expensive to pad and hanging it from the ceiling on a pulley looked shabby.

We found the old high chair, sterilized it, and stocked our shelves once again with little jars of baby food. Because of Sarah's ecological concerns, we rented cloth diapers and purchased pins guaranteed to draw blood from a diaper-changer's finger while fastening them one-handed. We even adopted Sarah and Charlie's dog, a wretched creature, so that it wouldn't be able to eat the baby out of jealousy.

When Chad started eating solid food, we replayed the

games we had used to get his mother to eat when she was a toddler. They worked no better than they had the first time. Chad preferred wearing his food to eating it. True, he made entertaining sounds and was positively amused by my efforts to convince him a spoonful of strained carrots was an airplane and his mouth a hangar. Chad showed artistic potential by the creative designs he drew in his green beans. I learned that out of the mouths of babes comes . . . cereal.

While allegedly eating, small boys sometimes manage not to spill food, although seldom. When crawling on the floor, babies will likely eat anything they find, dead or alive. While sitting, or in Chad's case, standing in a high chair, however, food becomes a plaything. Thus, to prevent malnutrition, I was reduced to sticking my fingers into the strained carrots and licking them in hopes that my grandson would do the same. Instead, Chad stuck them in his ears. I can't fault him for doing so, as my sampling of those carrots tasted a lot like earwax. Where two or three are gathered, and one of them is a year old, food is spilled.

A grandparent relearns that the secret of infant care is not only to keep one end filled but also to keep the other end dry. A baby reminds us that it is a changing world, several times a day. Ecology aside, paper diapers with easy-stick fasteners are a lot easier to use than cloth diapers and safety pins. This is particularly true if your grandson likes being naked and dry better than diapered and damp. And it helps little when his timing for, uh, evacuation comes in the middle of a change. At such moments the only solution is quiet patience and his grandmother who, like God, is a very present help in times of trouble.

In addition to the responsibilities of admiring, feeding, and changing a grandchild, the other main task is getting him to sleep. Parents establish routines with their children to which even small, active boys eventually conform. Instinctively, however, little children resist taking naps or going to bed at night when a grandparent is on duty. It becomes a test of wills.

Taking Chad for a walk in the stroller is one option. It succeeds as a way of lulling him to sleep if he wants it to work and thinks you need the exercise. It doesn't work if the grandfather is unable to walk less than five miles without stopping. Or if the dog thinks you're a kidnapper and barks one minute longer than it takes to awaken him. Middle-aged baby-sitters learn a cardinal rule, "Don't tire until you *can't* see the whites of his eyes."

Another option is taking the child for a ride in the car. Automobile manufacturers sometimes use scenes of parents driving small children through the countryside to sell their cars. The idea is that their machines are so restful and quiet, babies will happily fall asleep.

While this method works, it's imperfect. The journey of less than a thousand miles begins with a single step— the one a middle-aged man takes when he returns to the house to get the stuffed animal he's forgotten. The car seat is a safe and comfortable napping place, too, but removing a sleeping toddler from it is second only to brain surgery for delicacy and precision. Chad's car seat has a harness that, in addition to keeping him from bodily harm, could also protect an astronaut heading for Mars. Removing a small boy from it is, indeed, like performing surgery, and the main hope is that the anesthesia is still operative.

Grandbaby-sitters are, at best, second team players in the game of raising children. Good parents can overcome many of the mistakes an overanxious, semi-competent grandfather makes. The child, showing little discrimination, occasionally makes a grandparent's day by freely offering a smile or a hug.

Chad is surrounded by love, but it's clear that the primary loves are his parents, not the substitutes, as eager and adoring as they may be. That's gratifying. It's the way it should be. Carl Sandburg once said that "a baby is God's opinion that the world should go on." He, too, was a grandfather, and he saw that human love is passed along in families. It doesn't start with us. It doesn't end with us. We are participants in its passage, and, therefore, we are blessed.

22
WILL OUR CHILDREN HAVE FAITH?

When we reach middle age, we've either grown wiser or we're better able to hide our ignorance. We compensate for physical determination by a simpler set of desires. Most things we couldn't afford when we were young, we no longer want. If maturity begins after age fifty, it shows itself in how we view life. Mature people change from wishful thinking to thoughtful wishing. It's not guaranteed, of course. We're only young once, but we can stay immature all our lives.

What we wish for often becomes our legacy. Having grandchildren inspires us to fix a broken world for *their* sake. Noble living ought to be done for its own sake, but in middle age we may observe righteousness because we want to be well-remembered. We wonder, for what will my life be remembered?

As the dean of a seminary during a major capital campaign, I learned an important lesson about the desire to be remembered. One woman endowed the kitchen in our new building because she, when younger, often spent hours preparing food and providing hospitality for other people who were "taking care of the Lord's business." She saw her work as a legitimate part of the "Lord's business," too. She was right. Both Martha and Mary served Jesus.

Another widow underwrote a classroom in honor of her husband. She and her children wrote a citation in his memory. The citation included this sentence: "His family and friends hope that this room will become a place where other seekers like Tom can grow and search for the answers to their questions." His legacy was an encouragement to seekers after truth.

Christian people want to do more than take up space while they're alive. A characteristic of middle age is that we ponder more often than we did when we were twenty-five what we'll leave behind. Some are able to express their hopes in tangible ways, such as endowing a building or scholarship or cause that will live beyond their days. Most of us, however, simply hope that our time here will provide positive influences in the lives we've touched.

Conscientious parents wonder whether their words and examples affect their children. We know that some attitudes have been transmitted from *our* parents. Nancy often observes that she sounds just like her mother! My father's values included hard work, and to this day I can't rest until my work is done. We have to dig deep to bury our fathers.

Still, we never know for sure what gets passed along. There is always the possibility that we delivered messages that were misunderstood. Recall the joke about a Sunday school teacher who killed worms by dropping them in a glass of alcohol. Her intent was to provide an object lesson about the evils of liquor. She asked her class of fourth graders, "What did you learn?" One boy quickly responded, "If you want to get rid of worms, drink alcohol."

In our family we've tried to practice the Quaker testimony on simple living. The point, we thought, was clear. Money can't buy happiness. Our children agree, but they have also decided that money enables them to look for happiness in nicer places.

We regularly took them to church. (Quakers call it "Meeting.") We read the Bible with them. Youth group was their main social outlet, and they were blessed with excellent leaders who tried to teach their charges all they needed to know about God and morality—in one hour a week and without messing up the church basement. From the vantage point of middle age, we think their exposure to the Christian faith was at least similar, if not identical.

They're grown now. One of them is a faithful attender in a local congregation. Faithful living and religious understanding are a natural part of her adult life. Sarah is a better Quaker-Christian than her father.

Martha lives in Japan, and getting to a Christian church requires time and energy. Her faith is expressed in private worship, and her ethical behavior would make Jesus glad.

Our son conscientiously avoids worship, including Easter. He usually shows up on Christmas Sunday, particularly if special refreshments are being served.

Our youngest daughter delights in music, and she regularly attends wherever she is, especially if young men her age also appear.

They are, in other words, much like real people. When we reflect upon spiritual legacies we intended to pass along, it's clear they were incorporated by our children in varying degrees. That's usually the case for most families who embrace the Christian faith. Their children become selective embracers themselves. And, of course, so did we. If we claim to be Christian, half the pleasure in recalling our own spiritual past lies in the editing.

Ironically, the best legacy we can give our children is the stability of a two-parent home that works at being Christian. Yes, we know that many single parents nurture children into excellent adults, and they deserve blue ribbons for persistence and faithfulness. One-parent families who nurture their children as Christians are living examples of modern miracles. Nevertheless, the "Leave It to Beaver" family model is still the best hope for passing along faith and morality. The Bureau of Justice reports that 70 percent of the children who wind up in reform schools or jail grew up with one parent or none at all. The National Association of Elementary School Principals reports that 30 percent of children from two-parent homes become high achievers compared with 17 percent from one-parent families.

All families fall short of ideal results. Simply having two parents and avoiding police raids on our homes does not guarantee we pass along a legacy of faith. Faith and virtue are not caught like measles. Parents fall short. Families screw up. Nurturing faith is like doing a crossword puzzle with a fountain pen. The final result is darn hard to correct.

Nevertheless, the evidence is overwhelming that a two-parent family working hard at their faith commitments remains the best hope for a Christian legacy. If fathers desert their children and mothers resent both their husbands and the children, the odds against that legacy dramatically increase.

Middle age, when the nest is empty, provides perspective. It doesn't mean that our task of modeling the Christian faith is completed. We still have many spiritual miles to go before we sleep. Living the Christian life is like opening a new shirt. Whenever we think we've found all the pins, there's one left to stick us.

What we hope for is that we give Christian nurturing our best shot. Though imperfectly wrapped and not always of the highest quality, the gift has been given. If it was given with love, there is a chance it will be well received. After all, knowing we're loved is the best legacy of all. And being loved by one's family is still the best avenue for knowing we're loved by God.

23

THE COMFORT ZONE

Men and women who have been married for a long time can read each other's minds. They know in advance the other's opinions on the Soviet Union, who the next president should be, the weaknesses of last week's sermon, things present, and things to come.

Many husbands not only know but become dependent on their spouse's judgment on matters common or cosmic. Consider the following conversation Nancy and I had while having dinner in a friend's home.

Hostess:	"Would you like coffee or tea?"
Tom:	"I'd like hot tea."
Nancy:	"Tom, you know you don't like hot tea."
Tom:	"For a minute there I thought I did. Coffee, please."

Long-married spouses learn to honor each other's space. When, on vacation, Nancy becomes immersed in a five-hundred-page novel, I've learned from years of experience that interrupting her for any reason, including starvation, is grounds for divorce. Because she reads every word, instead of skip-reading as God intended, completing the book takes only slightly less time than writing it. Her family knows that she will eventually return to the real world and delight in how much her grandson has grown and that the Berlin Wall has been torn down.

She, in turn, has learned to honor the fact that basketball is more than a game to birthright Hoosers, and interrupting one on TV for any trivial cause, such as appendicitis, violates marital vows.

So when someone telephones, even long-distance, Nancy gives a standard reply: "I'm sorry, Tom can't come to the phone right now. He's in conference." And that's true. Usually it's the Big Ten, although occasionally it's the Atlantic Coast Conference. Long-married couples protect each other's space, no matter how spacey, and that's one of the reasons they're long-married.

Surprising as it is to young people, particularly their children, veteran couples continue to have romantic feelings for each other—even after fifty-five. True, they seldom kiss in public, and they usually turn the lights down low for economic, not romantic, reasons. Nevertheless, they share subtle pats, hugs, and looks that generate enough electricity to tingle but not electrocute.

Indeed, it is easy to understand love at first sight, but how do we explain it after two people have been looking at each other for thirty years or more? *June* and *moon* rhyme, but the September stage of a marriage doesn't necessarily imply fading passions. It implies contentment. George Jean Nathan once said that a man most truly loves a woman in whose company he can feel drowsy in comfort. Couples married thirty years no longer have to impress each other. Happy marriages begin when we marry the ones we love, and they blossom when we continue to love the ones we marry.

Familiarity breeds contentment. Romance after thirty years does not depend upon its own fires of passion to be sustained. It is nurtured by respect and forgiveness.

Long-married people have entered the comfort zone. Each stage of a relationship has its own inherent dangers, and the comfort zone is no exception. According to some social scientists, couples married a long time often flirt and fantasize to "cure fears, boredom, and a sudden sense of bodily decline." They may fall into the "haphazard, slow-motion lapse of a marriage slump."

Even so, the comfort zone can be invigorating and exciting. Long-term spouses know that marriage is a continuous process of dealing with the unexpected. Christians who believe that God calls them, sometimes, to change careers or follow a leading or act on a concern can respond to change without threatening their relationship: Had Isaiah been long-married, when the call came, "Whom shall I send and who will go for us?" he and his wife would have read each other's mind and said, "We'll follow if we can go together."

Couples don't get into the comfort zone just by growing older together. They only make it there by sharing beliefs and values, by listening together for God's call.

Becoming one in the Spirit just as they become one in the flesh is a key to reaching the comfort zone. Also, they don't deserve all the credit for making it there. Their chromosomes, their family environments, and the Christian communities of which they are part help a lot.

So, hurrah for young love, but contented sighs for life in the comfort zone. If we're able to enjoy the journey, the destination will be a time of joy and a place of peace.

24
VOCATIONAL TRAINING

Most middle-aged people know the value of work. Those of us fifty or older were Depression children, persons who grew up not long after nationwide bank failures, when unemployment was high and the ability to survive fragile. "Work hard so that you'll be secure" was the message.

My parents took that message seriously. They owned a small-town grocery–filling station, and they also had twelve acres of strawberries on the edge of town. My growing up years were filled with hard work, and I am still convinced my father grew strawberries primarily to provide work for his sons. He was good at it.

There are three ways to pick strawberries, and when there are twelve acres to harvest, all three ways are used. You can crawl, which eventually leads to calloused knees. Or you can squat as you pick strawberries, a practice—often forced on prisoners of war as punishment—that causes painful knots in the groin. Or you could bend from the waist, which leads to curvature of the spine. I have all three conditions today.

My father had found work that claimed the major portion of each school vacation. In the fall, over Thanksgiving vacation, we would put straw on the berries so they wouldn't freeze during the winter. Over spring vacation, we would remove the straw so that we could pick the berries over the late spring and early summer. Dad had carefully planted several varieties so that the picking season would be maximized. When they were picked and boxed, we would deliver them to the fruit markets. After the picking season, we would spend the summer cultivating the *!$&* berries.

Two insights came out of the experience which are important for my life. One, I was never going to earn my living growing strawberries, and gardening, to this day, is as welcome a hobby to me as pounding rocks on a chain gang. The other lesson that "took" was the belief that one's value as a person is tied to working hard, conscientiously, and well. That's why so many middle-agers are classic examples of the Puritan work ethic.

Many of us learn that it is important to work long hours six days a week and take few vacations. Otherwise, we won't be able to finance our heart attacks. But we also begin to wonder whether *work*, a four-letter word, is as important as we'd been led to believe.

For better or worse, a higher percentage of young

adults have already raised that question. Not being children of the Depression, they've benefited from more financial security than their parents. And more young adults, at least those who get married and have children, delight in the nurture of their offspring and value their relationships as husband and wife.

Whether that is an accurate generalization or not, from this fifty-six-year-old's perspective, it seems to be true. Looking at our lives now, *Meaning* is more important than successful productivity. Had I made a career out of raising strawberries, in other words, I would have immersed myself in doing that well. I would have found the best way of raising the biggest berries I could, berries so delicious they would win prizes at the fair, berries so large it would take only eleven to make a dozen. Of course, I would have expanded the operation and added acres under cultivation and acquired a fleet of trucks and . . .

It could have been a good life, particularly if I could have been in management and not have had to crawl, squat, and bend so much. Growing strawberries is a worthy vocation. The product is beautiful and you can stay close to the soil, particularly if you're picking the berries.

Whether successful or not, however, middle age causes many men and women to ask an important question about work. Do I still have enthusiasm? Does my work mean something important, not just to me, but to society?

Gail Sheehy discovered in 1974 that many persons, mostly men, were seeking a new pattern for their lives. They wanted to be connected with life at many levels. Commitment to family became more important and a desire to benefit society was highly valued. She called such persons *Integrators* in her best-selling book *Passages* (E. P. Dutton, 1974).

For the Christian who is middle-aged, such questions are expected outcomes of faithful living. After fifty-five, many of us think about retirement but not simply to take it easier. Instead, we think about being free to do other things, some of which are downright noble.

Seminaries around the country are full of former attorneys, businessmen and women, teachers, and others changing careers because they want their lives to be meaningful, and the ministry seems a means to that end. The irony is that many ministers are becoming lawyers, social workers, and teachers for similar reasons. There is no guarantee that there is more meaning on the other side of the fence, but seeking it is always the right thing to do.

Career changes and reassessments, of course, work best when we are financially independent. As we approach those decisions, we begin to wonder if we saved too little or lasted too long. Inflation gives even high-paying work a bad name. As a Quaker, when it comes to fighting inflation, I'm clearly a pacifist. And if we postpone our search for meaning until retirement, we may discover it's a time when our cup runneth under.

Whatever our decisions, middle age is more than simply a reward for not getting hit by a truck or dying from acne as a teenager. It is time to ask God, "What's next for me, Lord?" The answer may be, "More of the same. Keep on keeping on." Or we may leave our nets in the sea, and follow Him somewhere else.

If God calls, we respond. That part doesn't change with age. So seeking God's will is still our task. And if you've ever picked strawberries, your knees are ready.

25
THANKS, MOTHER

My mother was a product of her upbringing. Her father was killed in a farm accident when she was fourteen, and at eighteen she married a Hoosier who had migrated to Colorado where she lived. My parents owned and operated grocery stores and gasoline stations most of their lives, and Mother's careful frugality enabled the businesses to succeed.

In Kentland, Indiana, where I grew up, their store was called "First and Last Chance." Located on the edge of town, it provided the first chance to buy groceries coming into town from the west and the last chance to do so when going the other way.

We ate the vegetables and meat we couldn't sell, as Mother would trim away the spoiled parts and serve the rest for supper. My main after-school job was sacking potatoes, which consisted of filling ten-pound bags from hundred-pound bags. When you're only eight years old, thrusting a hand into a rotten potato gives existential meaning to the word *yucky* that lasts a lifetime.

Mother was small but tough. She was only about five feet two inches tall and delicate as a rose petal, but she worked fourteen-hour days between home and the family business. When Dad couldn't deliver gasoline to the chain of stations he serviced, Mother drove the huge truck up and down the hills of southern Indiana to make the deliveries.

Her discipline was simple and effective. I cannot recall ever being spanked by Mother, and she seldom raised her voice in anger. But she was clear in her expectations, and the look of disappointment in her eyes when we behaved badly was punishment worse than spanking. I report this authoritatively as Dad did not share Mother's aversion to corporal punishment, and opportunities to compare styles of discipline were abundant.

Going to church was one of those expectations, and by age twelve I had so many pins for perfect attendance attached to my suit jacket, I would have set off security alarms at any airport in the country—if there had been such devices in 1946 and if flying on an airplane would have been even a remote possibility. Mother taught Sunday school, was active in the Christian Women's Fellowship, served as an elder, and logged more time leading devotions at church meetings than many pastors. She read her Bible and prayed every day of her life. It was as natural as brushing her teeth.

Her faith sustained her the last two years of her life. When she learned she had cancer of the esophagus, she accepted that reality and went on taking care of business. The part she had the most difficulty understanding was the type of tumor she had. It was a kind of cancer that usually attacked people who were heavy smokers and/or drinkers. Mother had never smoked a single cigarette in her life, and if she had ever tasted alcohol, it was in cough medicine and she didn't know it. I teased her about "nipping on the side when nobody was looking," and she smiled and said it wasn't so.

Two weeks before Mother died, her granddaughter telephoned from Japan. Martha had called to say good-bye, but Mother worried that the call would be too expensive. She delighted in the hundreds of cards and letters she received, saving every one and savoring every word. One of her last requests was to make sure her church pledge be paid for the rest of the year.

In one sense Mother was not very modern. She couldn't understand why people were immodest or lazy or, worst of all, wasteful. Even though she had shared business ventures with Dad all her adult life, she thought a wife should primarily take care of her children and be supportive of her husband.

In another sense, however, she was very modern. She had two careers—one in business and the other as a parent. Mother never saw parenthood as an *imposed* role. Bringing up children "the way they should go" was a noble calling. As my brother and I remember her life, we honor her as "Mother," not as astute business manager or independent thinker, even though she was both.

Those able to be parents are doing significant work. Motherhood and fatherhood are not forms of second-class citizenship. The biological realities that allow women to *become* mothers—and men fathers—are secondary to the qualities of patience, love, and forgiveness that allow them to fulfill an essential calling—nurturing the next generation.

Any man or woman who has good parents has a better chance of being a good parent, too. Any man or woman who can demonstrate day after day what the Christian faith is *really* like has left a legacy that inspires others. It adds significance to life.

Good-bye, Mother. And thanks.

26
POSTSCRIPT

God sometimes goes out of the way to catch our attention. I may be a slow learner, but I guess I needed one more reminder that this middle-aged man has not yet resolved the puzzle of life.

There I was, happily "ripening" on my long-awaited sabbatical. I had been invited to speak at important conferences, at times feeling outrightly prestigious. My book, this one you're reading, was scheduled to reach the publisher by November 15. My life plan, for a change, was working.

Then "Adolf," as in Hitler, attacked. "Adolf" is the name I gave the virus that brought me down, quickly, for four weeks, including hospital time. My blood sugar went haywire. My colitis "boweled" me over. I lost my voice. I had to cancel speeches, miss appointments, delay tasks, and disappoint colleagues.

In twenty-five years at Earlham, I had never missed as many as ten days because of illness. My morale was lower than a snake's abdomen.

All the stuff middle age had brought to center stage had a new focus. We worry about our health after fifty. Was Adolf going to be a constant companion in the years ahead? In middle age we realize some dreams will not be fulfilled, but was I being warned that *none* of the best was yet to be? In this book, I'd tried to show that middle age brings wisdom and spiritual adaptability. Why then did I wonder if the last stage of life, just beginning, was retreat instead of anticipation?

The answer was obvious. I had forgotten what is always central in the Christian faith. There are no guarantees that old age or middle age or youth are going to be swell. What we are promised is that God, and the people of God, will walk with us.

All the evidence was there, but as I wallowed in my self-pity, I didn't see the signs. Christians don't function in isolation. They live connected to one another, sustaining, helping, supporting the one in need. It was my turn, and they were there.

The doctor who has treated my diabetes for twenty years did his usual lecture about health care, wrote a prescription that he thought would, finally, lick "Adolf," and then said, "I'll pray for you on Sunday." I learned that this good, kind, expensive doctor, a Roman Catholic, prays regularly, by name, for all his patients.

My children in New York and Japan called (not collect!) to see how I was doing. They lectured their mother about taking care of me, much the way Job yelled at God for not running the universe properly.

The doctor who had tenderly cared for my mother in her final days visited me in the hospital. A man of devout faith, he said he was making rounds anyway. I think he came just to encourage me.

When I had to cancel a speech, a colleague volunteered to substitute for me anytime he could. Alan is in remission from lymphoma, a disease that one day will take his life. He wanted to help because that's what brothers in Christ do.

The secretaries in my office, even though I was on sabbatical, screened my calls, protected my schedule, and made me sugar-free cookies. They cheered me and sympathized, but I realized they had been doing so for years. That's what sisters in Christ do.

Students, members of our congregation, men and women with whom we've walked when the night was dark—they said words and did deeds that created a cumulative spirit of love. The Apostle Paul described them a long time ago when he said that in the Body of Christ we rejoice and suffer together.

One conclusion, I suppose, is that all these people comforted me because I am wonderful. I would love to make that case, but the evidence is meager. And those comforters show no signs of limiting their care to middle-aged, diabetic Quakers.

The phrase *undeserved blessing* is a synonym for grace.

God's grace is the constant ingredient, available to all, and Christian people who listen and see can name it. It is not just friendship. It is not that we're recipients because we know the proper creedal formulas. Instead, it's a form of holding hands with God.

So, we live our lives in chapters, as my mentor, Elton Trueblood, is fond of saying. Middle age is one, and what comes later is another. Adolf has some evil kin waiting out there, so there's no guarantee that the next chapter will be pure fun. There is every reason to go forth with joy, however, because we walk arm in arm with brothers and sisters in Christ. I walk with Nancy, the legacies of parents and friends, the delight of our families, the promise of Chad and his soon-to-be-born cousin, and a great host of witnesses.

God, present as Spirit and also through persons who show God's presence, walks with us into the next chapter. We are not alone, even if we are lonely. And that is reason enough to go forth with joy.